Abrehet Mohammed Omer
A framework for Automatic Web Service
Composition based on service dependency analysis



TUDpress

Abrehet Mohammed Omer

# A framework for Automatic Web Service Composition based on service dependency analysis

TUDpress
2011

Gedruckt mit Unterstützung des Deutschen Akademischen Austauschdienstes

Bibliografische Information der Deutschen Nationalbibliothek
Die Deutsche Nationalbibliothek verzeichnet diese Publikation in der Deutschen Nationalbibliografie; detaillierte bibliografische Daten sind im Internet über http://dnb.d-nb.de abrufbar.

Bibliographic information published by the Deutsche Nationalbibliothek
The Deutsche Nationalbibliothek lists this publication in the Deutsche Nationalbibliografie; detailed bibliographic data are available in the Internet at
http://dnb.d-nb.de.

ISBN 978-3-942710-42-8


Verlag der Wissenschaften GmbH
Bergstr. 70 | D-01069 Dresden
Tel.: 0351/47 96 97 20 | Fax: 0351/47 96 08 19
http://www.tudpress.de


Gesetzt vom Autor.
Printed in Germany.

# A framework for Automatic Web Service Composition based on service dependency analysis

**Dissertation**

In partial fulfillment of the requirements of the degree
Doctor of Engineering (Dr.-Ing)

Submitted to
Technical University of Dresden
Department of Computer Science

by

**Abrehet Mohammed Omer**
born on 19.08.1976 in Assela

Advisors:

| | |
|---|---|
| Prof. Dr. rer. nat. habil. Dr. h. c. Alexander Schill | TU Dresden |
| Univ. Prof. Dr. Schahram Dustdar | TU Vienna |
| Prof. Dr. Uwe Aßmann | TU Dresden |

## Acknowledgments

First and foremost, I would like to thank my supervisor, Prof. Dr. rer. nat. habil. Dr. h. c. Alexander Schill, for allowing me to work under his chair. His consistent extraordinarily prompt near real-time feedbacks, constant follow-up, along with his scheduled nature forced me to always stick myself to schedules. His invaluable technical support is indispensable. I am very lucky to have the chance to work under his supervision.

I would like to thank my co-advisor Prof. Dr. rer. nat. habil. Uwe Aßmann, for his support during my research. I would like to express my gratitude to Univ.Prof. Dr. Schahram Dustdar for kindly agreeing to be my external reviewer.

Special thanks also go to Dr. Josef Spillner, Dr. Anja Strunk, and Dr. Iris Braun for their helpful ideas during the initial phase of the study. In particular, I am also indebted to Dr. Josef Spillner for his thoughtful comments on the original manuscript. I thank Dr. Waltenegus Dargie for proofreading this thesis and suggesting improvements to the language. All the feedbacks and comments I received have helped me in making of this thesis. I also enjoyed the time with my officemates Anne, Sandro, and Dong, I thank you for the accompany.

I have received enormous support from my family. My mother always has a special place in my life. She consistently encourages me to pursue my studies. I don't have words to express my love to her. She is the most intelligent woman in my life without formal education. My brother Jemal (Abi) have been my greatest mentor throughout my life, and I thank him from the bottom of my heart. My brothers and sisters, I owe you a big thank for your supports and love all along.

My daughters Liyou and Ruh, you always make me stop thinking about my research work with your irresistible smiles, which is the main source of my efficiency. Thinking of my beloved husband Negede always keep me strong. He was with me all along the study period, being my motivator, critic, reviewer, and above all, the best partner one can ever dream. His presence, at happy and hard times, and invaluable moral and technical help were instrumental to the conduct of my research. Thanks are also due to all my friends living in Germany for making me feel home and made my life complete. I should also express my appreciation to my friends who supported me via technology.

Last but not least, very special thanks goes to the DAAD (Deutsche Akademischer Austausch Dienst) in providing the financial support to this PhD study.

# Contents

# Figures

# List of Algorithms

# Tables

# ABSTRACT

The practice of composing web services has received an increasing interest with the emerging application development architecture called Service Oriented Architecture (SOA). A web service composition can be done either manually or (semi-) automatically. Doing composition (semi-) automatically minimizes runtime problems that arise due to dynamic nature of runtime environments. However, the implementation of (semi-) automatic composition demands for the automation of a process model or a composition plan generation process. In addition, creating a composite service or applications from component services, that are developed and meant to work independently, causes unavoidable dependencies among the services involved. Consequently, in a composite service development, understanding, analyzing and tracking of such dependencies becomes important. This thesis views the process model generation sub-task of a service composition as a service dependency identification and analysis problem.

In this thesis, we propose a dependency based automatic process model generation methods. For this purpose, the following issues are explored. First, a top layer architecture with a composition engine is developed. The architecture gives a complete picture of dependency based automatic service composition. Second, the process model generation sub-task is formulated as a service dependency identification and analysis problem. Third, a two-stepped method for automatic process model generation, given a set of candidate web service descriptions, is proposed.

The first step of the proposed approach deals with the identification of potential direct and indirect dependencies between abstract services. The direct dependency extraction is done by assuming a semantic I/O matching of service parameters. The extraction of indirect dependency from direct dependency is done using a recursive algorithm derived from the transitive closure property. Alternatively the Warshall algorithm is used.

The second step of the proposed approach deals with analysis of dependency information and generation of process model (PM) automatically. To execute this step, we propose two approaches: matrix based and graph based approaches. The matrix based approach utilizes both direct and indirect dependencies. This approach represents dependencies using matrix and takes advantages of a sorting algorithm. The matrix representation facilitates a simplistic mathematical dependency analysis for generating important indicators during automatic process model creation. The process model is generated using a sorting algorithm that uses the analysis result obtained from the dependency matrix as sorting criterion. The graph based approach uses only direct dependency among candidate services. As its name indicates, in this approach the extracted I/O dependencies are represented using a directed graph. A modified topological sorting algorithm is used for generating a process model that shows the execution order of candidate services. Both of the proposed approaches (matrix and graph based approaches) recognize the existence of cyclic dependencies and provide ways of dealing with them. The resulting process model or composition plan from both approaches has a sequential, concurrent and loop control flows.

Finally, the performance of the proposed approaches is studied theoretically as well as experimentally. For the experimental validation and evaluation purpose, the approaches are implemented in a prototype that facilitates the validation and evaluation of the approaches at a larger scale. An extensive experimental performance evaluation is done first on each proposed approach. The two approaches are then compared and their pros and cons under different scenarios are assessed.

# Chapter 1

# Introduction

This introductory chapter presents the research motivation, the research objectives and the problems that are addressed. In addition, the research approach and its scope as well as the research contributions and the organization of the thesis are presented.

## 1.1 Background

Service composition is the process of combining and linking available component services to create a composite service that has more functionality than the component services it is made of. A composite service can be regarded as a combination of services invoked in a predefined order and executed as a whole. It is used in situations where a client request cannot be satisfied by any single available service.

The service composition process comprises the following major sub activities:

1. *Process model (composition plan) creation*: a process model is a model that simplifies the representations of activities and their enactment. It specifies the full task control- and data-flow among different subtasks. It can be done manually (by a developer at design time), semi-automatically (with the help of a template) or automatically (by a software agent).

2. *Concrete service discovery and binding*: this activity involves finding and bind-

ing services for each subtask of the composite service. It can be done at design time or run time.

3. *Availing composite service*: this refers to making the composite service available to a potential client and its management.

A service composition could be done statically, semi-dynamically or dynamically (fully automated). These different levels of automation are determined by how and by whom the process model is created and the timing (design or run time) of service discovery and binding. In static composition, a process model is created manually and a service binding is done at design time. Whereas in a dynamic composition a process model is created automatically and a service binding is done at runtime. All methods in between these two extremes are categorized as semi-dynamic [2] (see figure 2.2).

Static service composition has shortcomings in that it does not adapt automatically unpredictable changes in a dynamic run time environment. For example, new services might become available, old services might be inaccessible, or a number of service providers might grow or shrink. Under such circumstances a composite service requires a run time adaptation which cannot be achieved by a static service composition. Due to such shortcomings of static composition methods nowadays there is a growing tendency for shifting to a dynamic service composition mechanisms. A dynamic service composition composes services on-demand, without or with minimum user intervention. It has the following advantages: It enables composite application extension at runtime, it does not need to keep a local repository of available web services, and it is possible to produce more than one composite service with the same set of component services [3]. In the endeavor of shifting from a static to a dynamic service composition, many approaches achieve a semi-dynamic composition. One that realizes the runtime service binding while still relying on a manual process model creation, is for example, the work by [4, 5]. However, realizing a dynamic service composition or tackling the problems a static composition mechanisms are not only limited to achieving a runtime service binding but they also demand the ability to automatically creating a process model.

In a few cases, where attempts were made for creating fully-dynamic composition mechanisms, researchers tried to tackle the problem by mixing the process model creation and the service binding process into one. In this regard, the work by [6, 7, 8] can be mentioned. Such methods implement an automated chaining of services or a graph representation of available services. The main limitation with this kind of approaches is scalability. Specially, simple chaining methods may insert a high degree of uncertainty regarding semantic correctness and the search space is very large [9]. Moreover, the algorithms can execute indefinitely if matches are not found, or may result in compositions of too many component services [10].

The most extensively employed attempts towards a fully dynamic composition which includes an automatic process model creation is a planning based technique adopted from Artificial Intelligence (AI). For example, a body of work by [11, 12, 13] use GOLOG with AI planning technique and a work by [14] use case-based reasoning from AI machine learning techniques. The AI planning approaches for service composition has scalability and high computation time requirement as limitations [15][2]. Moreover, these techniques require a complete knowledge about the existing services and their transition. Building a complete knowledge base takes a considerable time and space with a fast growth of web services. Also the performance of AI planning algorithms is significantly influenced by the size of the knowledge base. As a result most of AI based composition techniques begin with a closed world assumption.

From the discussion above it is apparent that the complexity of creating a process model automatically is the main bottle neck for achieving a dynamic service composition. It is the major missing link in the road leading to achieving a fully dynamic web service composition and thus is the focus of this research.

A thorough investigation of the approaches in a process model creation shows that all methods try to extract implicit or explicit dependencies (relationships) while they try to create composite services. For example, in graph-based and chaining mechanisms, while trying to create a process model, mainly input/output relationships between services are explicitly searched in their algorithm. In workflow based techniques programmers try to identify implicit and explicit dependencies. In case of AI-based methods input/output, temporal and some other logical relationships are considered by making use of domain knowledge.

Though the concept of dependency is explored in component based systems, principally for managing component based systems [16, 17], there are some approaches that recognize the importance of dependency in SOA, specifically in a service composition. For example, [18] looks at service dependencies from a composite service management point of view. In their approach, it is shown that dependencies could be tracked from log files, which normally are available in SOA audit files. [19] discusses the use of dependency information from composite services to establish a dependency-aware service-oriented architecture. Its main aim is to capture and reuse composite service information, which is called service dependency, for further composition. The service dependency in [19] principally refers to a temporal dependency in order to determine the sequential execution path.

[20, 21, 22], use a pre-computed dependency graph between all services in a repository. These approaches utilize back-ward chaining and graph search algorithms to find a sub-graph that contains services that are teaming to accomplish the requested task. The dependency graph size becomes very complex when there is a high number of services in the repository, which probably increases the complexity of the algorithm of the composition plan creation. Moreover, they assume the dependency graph to be an acyclic graph which, however, is not always true in reality.

As mentioned above a dynamic service composition has many advantages. However, it also has some disadvantages and limitations, especially when the composition problem is complex, in which case the composition becomes difficult to achieve. This limits its wide application in real world situations. This limitation could be overcomed by resorting to a semi-dynamic composition techniques but those with high degree of automation during a process model creation to speed up the composition process [2]. The advantage of resorting to such technique is that they could use available static knowledge (i.e. advertised abstract service description), which is left out by most of dynamic service composition mechanisms that would otherwise support the process of service composition. Their advantage over the mere semi-dynamic composition methods is their automation in the process model creation which eliminates the burden of a manual process model creation and increase the flexibility of creating composite service on demand.

Therefore, this thesis focuses, first, on a general framework for automatic service composition using extracted dependency from a statically available knowledge about services; second, on establishing automatic process model creation methods that are solutions to one of the main problems, to increase the automation level of service composition techniques. The automatic process model generation methods utilize automatically extracted service dependency that has not been adequately addressed in earlier and recent researches. This is considered as a step forward towards semi-dynamic composition with a high degree of automation in a process model creation. Furthermore, a prototype that has a test bed to enable test and validation of a service composition techniques is developed and used to validate the proposed approaches.

## 1.2 Motivation

Though there are various existing techniques of service composition, there are still open issues and limitations that need to be addressed. In particular this research is inspired by the following issues:

1. The need to have (semi-) dynamic-composition technique to overcome limitations of static-composition techniques.

2. The importance of automatic process model creation to achieve dynamic composition and the fact that this is a missing link in the endeavor of shifting from static to dynamic composition.

3. The relationship between process model creation and service dependency and its potential for use in automatic process model creation.

In this research service dependency is treated as a core concern for dynamic service composition. This is because understanding dependencies between services is a requirement to automatic process model creation.

## 1.3 Problem statement and primary research objectives

As it is described in section 1.1 there are many issues and knowledge gaps that hinder the transition towards achieving a dynamic composition. Specifically, the lack of runtime process model creation techniques complicates the intent for a (semi) dynamic service composition. In earlier researches the usage of service dependency among component services for an automatic process model creation was not significant. Therefore, there is a clear research need to understand service dependency and get more refined means to identify, represent, analyze, and use service dependency information for ultimate use in an automatic process model creation. Consequently, developing methods for an automatic dependency extraction and an automatic process model creation will be the main research problem.

More specifically, the main issues that this thesis addresses can be summarized with the following research questions :

1. How can statically available knowledge be used to achieve a (semi) dynamic service composition?
2. How can dependencies among component services comprising a composite service be efficiently and automatically determined?
3. How to generate an appropriate process model for composite services using service dependency information?

Thus the primary objectives of the research, are:

1. To develop a general architectural frameork that provides a complete picture of

a dependency based automatic web service composition technique.

2. To identify the general web service dependency types.

3. To develop a methodology for extracting dependencies among web services.

4. To get a way of representing and analysing web service dependencies for further use.

5. To show the application of web service dependency for an automatic process model or a composition plan* generation.

## 1.4 Scope and approach

The service dependency based automatic service composition discussed in this thesis pre-supposes that there exists a formal user request, statically available local repository, with abstract service description, and a goal based service discovery mechanism. The goal based service discovery mechanism is responsible for discovering and selecting the component services that could satisfy a user request that can not otherwise be satisfied by a single service. The discovery and selection of services is made from local repository of services. In fact, goal based service discovery mechanisms are mainly used in individual service discovery web services for a specific request, such as [23] and [24]. Goal based service discovery mechanism is out of the scope of this research.

Therefore, the starting ground for the proposed approach is a formal user request and selected abstract service descriptions that are ready for composition.

---

*In this thesis process model and composition plan are used interchangeably

The proposed approach principally focuses on automatically identifying and analyzing service dependency among component services and then making it ready for use in process model creation.

To achieve the specific goals mentioned in section 1.2 and to ultimately solve the main research question, the research follows seven major steps. The steps are:

1. Identifying the common web service dependency types in service composition;
2. Establishing a methodology to identify and specify dependencies among web services;
3. Selecting a way to represent and analyze web service dependencies for further use;
4. Illustrating the application of web service dependency for a process model generation;
5. At the end of the conceptual work, a prototype is developed to demonstrate the proposed strategies. To validate and evaluate its potentials and limitations different case scenarios are considered.

## 1.5 Research contributions

The main contributions of this research is proposing dependency based automatic process model creation techniques for the purpose of dynamic composition. Moreover, a prototype that has a composition engine developed using the proposed approach is implemented. The prototype is capable of generating synthetic composable web services with similar behavior as existing web services in order to validate and evaluate the proposed methods.

As a whole the contributions can be summarized as follows:

1. To the best of our knowledge, this research is the first to give an on-demand process model creation based on dependency that is extracted automatically from an abstract service description. It also shows the use of indirect dependencies for a composition plan generation. Moreover, the developed approach is capable of extracting dependency automatically. This capability is useful not only in process model creation but also in a SOA management.

2. Despite most methods that use service dependency for a composition plan creation [22, 25, 21], the approach in this thesis does not pre-compute unnecessary semantic links between all registered services. We argue that finding out only the semantic link (dependency) among candidate abstract service descriptions for the required composition avoids the unnecessary computation required to create all links between services in the registry. Moreover, the use of abstract service description that represent a collection of services with the same functionality minimizes the search space in the local repository.

3. To the best of our knowledge, the approach proposed by this research is the first to deal with cyclic dependency in detail. The proposed approach is capable of finding cyclic dependencies from the generated dependency; it is illustrated that what cyclic dependency means, how cyclic dependency can be used as an indicator of a loop control flow and how to eliminate it to avoid further complexity in a further execution plan generation process.

4. It proposes the use of simple sorting and topological sorting algorithms for generating a process model. This solves the scalability problems that occur in many composition plan generation algorithms.

5. The research develops a prototype validation system that generates synthetic web services using random parameters, which can be used to test other approaches of web service composition in a closed world assumption.

## 1.6 Structure of the thesis

Apart from the introduction in chapter 1, the thesis is composed of the following parts.

The basic concepts and terminologies are presented in chapter 2. Moreover, an extensive review of related work is given. The review is done separately for different categories of service composition techniques which are introduced in the first chapter.

Chapter 3 focuses on elaborating the proposed approach from different perspectives. Section 3.1 introduces the composition problem from the perspective of the thesis. Section 3.2 presents the way services, user request, service dependency and composite services are specified. In section 3.3 a small motivating scenario to show a brief overview of the proposed approach is provided. In section 3.4 the proposed architecture along with explanation of each part of the architecture is presented. Section 3.5 presents the summary and conclusion of the chapter.

Chapter 4 presents the automatic dependency extraction process and a description of an example scenario. In section 4.1, the description of a complex example scenario, which will be used throughout the thesis for illustrating the proposed methodologies, is presented. In section 4.2 a detail explanantion of the automatic dependency extraction method is given.

Chapter 5 describes a matrix-based approach to create a composition plan automatically. The chapter starts by providing a matrix based method to manage a cyclic dependency which is consdiered the first step of the approach. Then continues the process model generation which is based on Topological sorting algorithm.

In chapter 6 a graph-based approach to create a composition plan automatically is presented. The chapter starts by providing a graph based method to manage a cyclic dependency which is based on the Tarjan algorithm. Then follows the composition plan generation which uses a modified topological sorting algorithm.

In chapter 7, a prototype implementation and an evaluation of the proposed approach is described. Here the description of implemented prototype and the experimental results are presented in detail.

Finally, in chapter 8 conclusions and outlooks for future research work is provided.

# Chapter 2

# Background and related works

This chapter has two parts. The first part provides a brief introduction to basic concepts of Service Oriented Architecture (SOA), service dependency and other related concepts with the intention of giving background knowledge on service composition techniques. The second part provides a review of selected works related to this research. The related works section has four sub sections. In 2.2.1 reviews of related work on component and service dependency are presented. In section 2.2.3 review of service composition approaches, categorized based on the automation level and consideration of service dependency usage, is discussed. Finally, in section 2.2.4 a summary and comparison of related works is given.

## 2.1 Background

### 2.1.1 Service Oriented Architecture (SOA) concepts

Service Oriented Architecture (SOA) is an application development architecture that uses individual software services to build composite applications. This is possible because smaller and simpler applications can be developed and availed in the form of Web Services (WS). These individual applications can be published, located, and invoked across the web. The ability to invoke and compose services using multiple individual services allows meeting larger and single user requirements, which could not otherwise be met with any of the available smaller services. Thus, a complex service based applications can be created in a SOA environment by composing individual services. This application development architecture (SOA) has increased the demand for web services and it has called for researches in the area of WS composition.

In SOA there are three major actors involved: the service provider, service requester and web broker. Each actor has different responsibilities involves around the services. Service providers develop web services and make them accessible to service consumer. Service requesters (consumers) get the service by sending request in a specified manner. Service broker is a mediator between provider and requester.

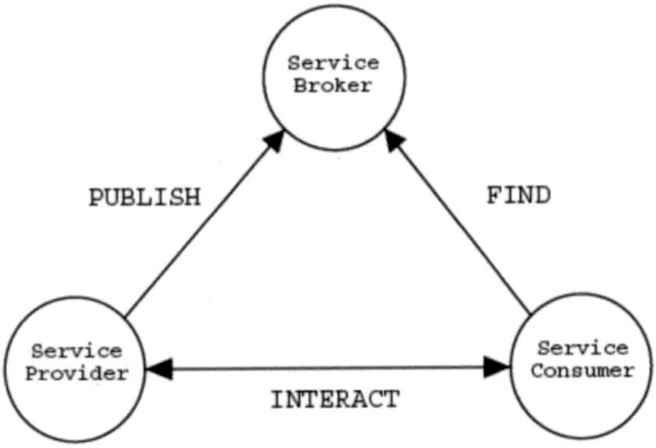


Figure 2.1 : The Service Oriented Architecture [1]

web services are the fundamental block of SOA. Web Services (WSs) are self-contained, modular units of application logic, which provide business functionality to other applications/users via an Internet connection. WSs are not dependent on the context or state of other web services. The development process of web services has become sufficiently mature [26]. At present more and more small and simple applications are being developed and made available in the form of WS. As a result developers/researchers start working towards other potential usage of web services like developing applications making use of existing web services.

Since Web Services (WS) have main role in service oriented architecture we need to explore and understand them. i.e. it is important to know how they are designed (web service description), how they can be accessible to consumer (web service discovery), how they can interact and accomplish a bigger task that can not be accomplished by a single service (web service composition). The next sub section describes these basic concepts.

### Web Service description

Web Service description is important for clients to understand and use a service provided. It is necessary because the communication between WS requester and provider should be in an orderly manner. Web services can be described by their functional and non-functional properties. Functional property description provides what exactly the service can do in the form of input, output, pre-condition and effect. Non-function property description gives anything a service gives as a constraint over the functional properties such as: cost, computation time, response time etc. A service consumer must understand each service in-terms of functional and non-functional properties in order to communicate and get appropriate result from web services.

There are different technologies for describing services. Different technologies have different description capabilities. Web service description technologies categorized by application domain and presented in [27]. In this paper syntactic, semantic and resource description languages are provided. In syntactic web service description category web service description language (WSDL) and web service business process execution language (WS-BPEL) are mentioned. WSDL describes only requirements and capabilities of web services [28]. It provides only a comprehensive technical description of a service. WS-BPEL is used to define an executable business process than individual services [29]. It focuses on describing state transitions and interaction of processes making use of WSDL description for message exchanges. Technologies like semantic web service description language-S (WSDL-S) [30], semantic annotation for web service description language (SA-WSDL) [31], web service ontology language (OWL-S) [32], web service modeling ontology (WSMO) [33], web service modeling language (WSML) [34] are being discussed in semantic Web service community.

WSDL-S extends WSDL by defining new elements and annotations for already existing elements. It connects WDSL and OWL. OWL[32] is a W3C standard based on resource description language (RDF)(S) and it has been designed to meet the need for a web ontology language. OWL-S is an ontology represented in OWL which contains a bunch of classes and property definitions. SA-WSDL is based on WSDL-S and provides semantic characterization to Input and Outputs of web services by defining a small set of WSDL extension attributes. WSMO provides a conceptual model necessary for semantic web services. It includes: goals, ontologies, mediators and functional semantic description of web services. WSML describes WS in the form of ontologies. It is a way to formally describe components in WSMO. Such semantic descriptions could help in enhancing existing service composition techniques and in developing new automatic service composition mechanisms that involve the usage of semantic knowledge in the composition process. In general, semantic web description creates another layer on the top of WS infrastructure to supply semantic meaning to web services. To fully utilize WS users (service consumers) should be able to discover, compose and synthesize services automatically. For that a proper WS description is necessary.

Once the WS developed and described in proper manner service providers register it to service registry located on web broker and consumers search for it in the registry using the WS description. What follows after WS description is WS discovery by service consumer.

### Web Service discovery

WS discovery is related to getting appropriate service for a request. It is one of the critical steps in the process of developing applications based on SOA. It can be done using syntactic matching or semantic matching.

[35] presents a method to locate required web services on the basis of the capabilities that they provide. i.e semantically enabled I/O matching a technique. Their strategy tries to accommodate a softer definition for the term 'sufficiently similar' ( i.e makes the matching techniques flexible since in real case scenario no exact match can always be found ). For such flexibility in the algorithm different degree of matching is defined. To do this, whenever a match between the request and any of the advertisements is found, it is recorded and stored to find the matches with the highest degree. [36] also used the degree of matching proposed by [35] and extend it by adding intersection function.

### Web Services composition

The other fundamental concept is web service composition which sometimes overlaps or will merge with the process of WS discovery. WS composition is a mechanism of combining two or more basic services into a possibly complex service. It is used to solve complex problems by combining available basic services. It helps to accelerate rapid application development and facilitate service reuse from developer perspective and from user perspective it increases complex service consumption. As mentioned earlier a composite service can be regarded as a combination of services invoked in a predefined order and executed as a whole and that has more functionality than its components. WS composition is needed because finding a right service provider for the request is not an easy task on fast growing WWW sometimes it is even impossible. Thus WS composition becomes necessary and inevitable. Composing WS from existing ones is an effective method to fill this gap.

There are different WS composition techniques developed by researchers. These techniques are also categorized based on various criteria. For example: [2] categorized the techniques into three major categories, static, semi-dynamic and dynamic, based on the way process model created and the time of service binding as shown in figure 2.2. [3] provide six categories(runtime reconfiguration using wrappers, runtime component adaptation, composition language, work-flow-driven composition techniques, ontology-driven web service composition and declarative composition) of dynamic service composition techniques based on the underlying approach. [37] presents a survey of WS composition techniques from the work-flow and AI planning research community. This thesis uses the classification made by [2] and further classify the methods based on the underlying approach used in their algorithm and the way their process

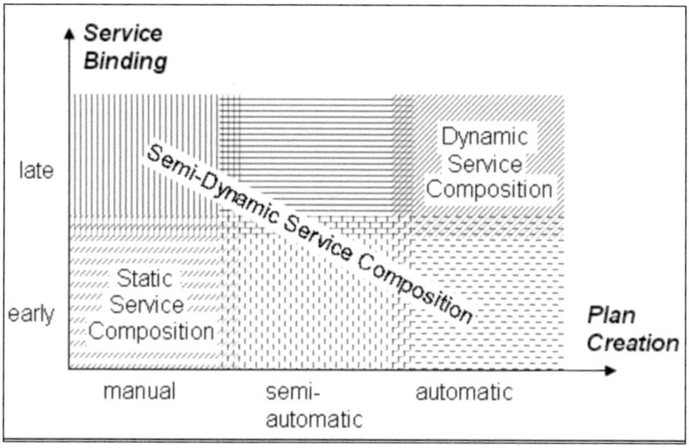


Figure 2.2 : Classification of WS composition techniques[2]

model is created. In section 2.2 review of related work based on such categorization is presented.

### 2.1.2 Service dependency

In SOA the task of creating composite services from component services results dependencies between the component services. Primarily these services are created by same or different providers and they are meant to be accessed and work independently. However, establishment of composite services necessitates interaction, communication, cooperation and coordination of services and this inevitability create some sort of dependencies among the services.

As described in chapter 1, the course of action of process model creation in various service composition techniques involves tracing directly or indirectly various type of dependencies among web services. Similarly, our approach also begins from extracting dependency between services to create execution plan for composite service.

### Overview of dependencies

There are different kinds of service dependencies among component services within a composite service. One can identify the possible service dependencies from data and control flows, which occur due to the need for interaction among component services in composite service. The following dependency types are the most common among many:

1. Sequential control flow occurs due to data (I/O) or temporal dependency caused by user constraints. I/O dependency happens when the data generated by one service should be used by another service. (For example if a user requests to book boat trip or buy movie ticket depending on weather condition then weather forecast data generated by weather services will be used by the two services book boat trip and buy movie ticket services).

2. Concurrent control flow happens when there is no dependency between services.

3. Loop control flow happens due to repetition (cyclic) dependency. Cyclic dependency occurs when a service is dependent on it self or when there exits a cycle of dependency chain.

4. Alternative control flow is used in relation to selection dependency. Selection dependency occurs when there is a criteria set for selecting among services, for

example when a criteria is satisfied then select service A otherwise select service B. From the example considered above, if weather is good go book Boat tour else buy movie ticket. It can also occur if service A costs less than service B but with the same functionality which are called alternative services.

There are also other types of dependencies which can not be explicitly attached to any of existing control flows that are normally used in composite service execution plan generation. For example, when a service uses another service in order to complete its task (eg. credit card payment service may require validation service before it completes the payment process).

The focus of this thesis is the first three types of dependency and the approach can generate a process model with sequential, concurrent and loop control flow.

## 2.2 Related work

The two major research topics relevant to this thesis are service dependency and service composition. These two research topics are very broad and inter-related. Figure 2.3 gives pictorial description of their inter-relation. This section gives review on works related to service dependency and service composition. In addition, it gives and comparison of existing composition techniques.

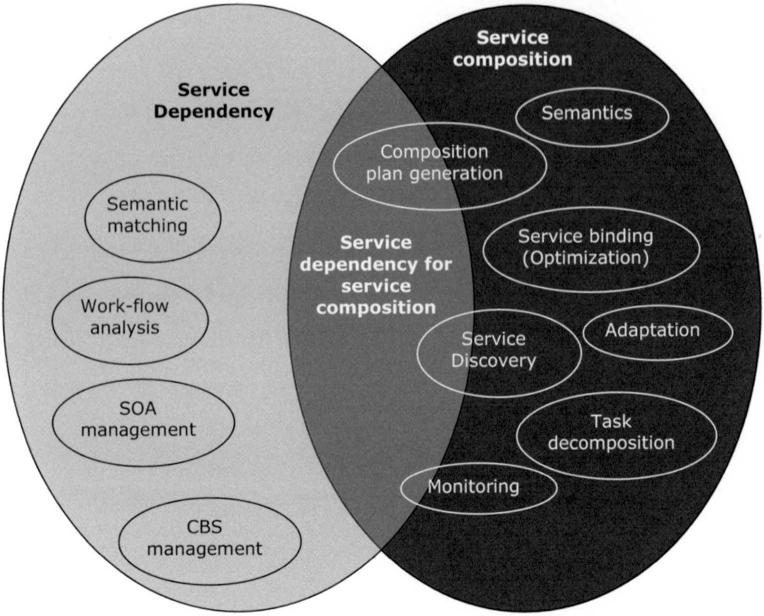


Figure 2.3 : State of the art

### 2.2.1 Service dependency

Dependency information is seen being used both in component based systems and SOA. Brief overview of published work about dependency that bears a relation to our work is given here.

[16] discussed the use of component dependency in component-based software engineering. They proposed a matrix based method to analyze dependencies in component-based software engineering. In their approach dependencies are represented by graph,

which can equivalently be represent by an adjacency matrix. Ultimately, they discussed how dependency analysis result can be used to understand, test and to maintain component based systems. The approach in this thesis also uses adjacency matrix and directed graph to represent service dependency.

Another work by [19] discusses the possibility of deploying and reusing composite services based on service dependency. In their research, the composite service is described in terms of elementary service dependency extracted from a pre-existing process model. The invocation of the composite services is done by managing these dependencies. Their goal is to create dependency aware service interaction, i.e. dependency aware service publication, discovery, composition and binding.

[18] looks for service dependencies from a composite service management point of view. Their approach shows that dependencies could be tracked from log files, which normally are available in SOA audit files. Here, dependencies are utilized for impact analysis (to distinguish services that can be affected by a particular service status) and service-level root-cause analysis (finding out the reasons of a service failure by inspecting at the other services it depends on).

[38] identifies primary service dependencies and model them by graph. Then generates a dependency matrix that specify the degree of dependency among services. Using the information from dependency analysis modeled by matrix and graph, they developed an impact analysis model that looks at the impact of the service evolution. In this paper the concept of cyclic dependency is not mention.

### 2.2.2 Dependency based service composition techniques

Most of the approaches that use dependency graph for composition utilizes chaining algorithms, for instance [21] and [20] can be mentioned. Chaining algorithms try to find the link between service input and output parameters in order to create a process model that satisfies the user request. Forward chaining begins from input or pre-condition of user request and searches for chain of services till it reaches output or final goal of the user request. The backward chaining follows the same procedure in opposite direction, i.e. it starts from output of user request and ends at the input of user request.

[21] proposes to pre-compute and store network of services that are linked by their I/O parameter. The link is built by using semantic similarity functions that is based on an ontology. They represent the service network using graph structure. Their approach utilizes back-ward chaining and depth-first search algorithms in order to find a sub-graph that contains services to accomplish the requested task. Unlike [22] they propose a way to select optimal plan in cases when more than one plan is found.

[22] used dependency graph to store information about existing web services in repository. In the graph, nodes represent I/O parameters and edges represent web services. Web services are modeled using I/O description and dependency information to other WSs through its I/O. They utilize graph search algorithm to find set of candidate services for the composite service. They also use interface automata tool to create execution path by taking discovered services. They did not discuss a way to stop search of candidate services. This possibly makes search complicate in cases when more than one set of candidate service exist. The complexity of their approach is

exponential in terms of the number of involved parameters, and also exponential in terms of the number of services in a repository.

In [20], the authors propose dependency graph based web service composition. In their graph structure nodes characterize both I/O parameters and services, while edges characterize the link among parameter nodes and service nodes. The graph construction is done in a way that facilitates the use of backward chaining algorithm, i.e. the edge starts from output parameter node, goes to service name node and then to input parameter node. In order to get the required services for a composite task they use back-ward chaining, in combination with depth first search, . They did not clearly discuss execution plan generation algorithm and the complexity.

However [20, 21, 22] generates (pre-computed) dependency graph between all services in repository. This procedure complicates and makes the graph size very big when there is high number of services. They do selection of candidate services based on pre-computed dependency graph.

[39], [40] and [41] uses Service Dependency Graph(SDG) and AND/OR graph in their proposed approaches. The SDG is formed from data and service nodes. An edge could be either from data node to service node or vice-versa or from data to data node. An edge from data node to service node implies that data is an input for the service and an edge from service to data implies that data is an output of the service. An edge is from data to data node implies that one is sub class of the other. When there is a directed path from one service node to another through data node then there is dependency between those services. Based on some simple logical rules AND/OR graph constructed from SDG is used in their proposed algorithm. Their algorithm gives a sub-graph of the AND/OR graph or SDG as solution for composition problem.

There is no major semantic difference between SDG and AND/OR graph. In an AND/OR graph the data nodes are represented as OR nodes. This indicates that data can be output of either of the source service nodes. In an AND/OR graph the service node is represented as AND node. The implication is all source nodes (data nodes) for incoming edges to-wards service (AND) node is pre-requisite for a service to start execution. [39],[40] and [41] has used the extracted dependency information for automatic service composition. However, in their graph representation existence of cyclic dependency is not included.

The main difference among the approaches, discussed above, is in the representation of service dependency and in the algorithm utilized to generate a composite service. They all assume the dependency graph to be acyclic, which is not always true in reality. In case of cycle existence their composition algorithm fails.

In [42] a service composition technique that utilizes Casual Link Matrix(CLM) is presented. CLM is used to store semantic I/O link between candidate services. The CLM is built based on semantic similarity functions that provide the degree of similarity between input and output parameters of web services. To generate the composition plan, they use a recursive and regression-based search AI planning technique. They claim that the complexity is polynomial time in number of rows, number of columns, which is equivalent of number of I/O parameters. They explicitly mentioned that the approach fails when cycle is detected.

Table 2.1 summarizes the various approaches that use dependency with respect to five aspects. The table shows the way dependencies are modeled(graph or matrix); whether semantics is used or not(yes/ no); whether cyclic dependency are considered or not (yes/ no); whether the approach assumes closed world assumption or not (yes/

no) and in the comment column it gives the application area in which dependencies are utilized.

Table 2.1 : Summary table of dependency usage

| Year | Author | Modeling method | Semantic usage | Cyclic dependency | Closed world | Comment |
|---|---|---|---|---|---|---|
| 2005 | B. Li et al. | Matrix and Graph | no | no | NA | In CBS |
| 2006 | L. Ma et al. | Matrix | no | no | NA | In CBS |
| 2007 | J. Zhou et al. | NA | NA | - | NA | Dependency aware SOA |
| 2007 | S. Basu et al. | NA | NA | no | NA | Service impact analysis in composite service |
| 2007 | R. Aydogan et.al | Graph | | no | no | Service composition |
| 2008 | Z. Gu | Graph | no | no | no | Service composition |
| 2005 | D. B. Claro et al. | Matrix | NA | NA | NA | Service discovery optimization |
| 2006 | F. Lecue and A. Leger | Matrix | yes | no | yes | Regression based automatic composition |
| 2009 | S.Wang, et al. | Matrix and Graph) | NA | NA | NA | For Service evolution (Version) |
| 2005 | S. V. Hashemian, et.al | Graph | no | no | no | Automatic service composition |
| 2008 | H. N. Talantikite | Graph | yes | no | no | Automatic service composition |

CBA=Component Based System

NA=Not Applicable

### 2.2.3 Service composition approaches

In this section, we review some web service composition approaches by focusing on the way they formulate the composition problem and create composition plan. The review is made by classifying the approaches based on the level of automation the composition process (see figure 2.2). A more extensive study of web service composition approaches can be found in the survey articles [37, 3, 9, 43].

#### Static composition approaches

Static service composition approaches are sometimes called work-flow based methods. [44] presents a static composition techniques that abstracts web services. They claim the abstraction is useful to present web services interfaces and operations in a consistent and uniform manner. The process model is created manually from set of candidate services collected from the local library that stores the abstracted web services.

[45] provides a work-flow editor to compose from distributed data sources. It allows scientists to effectively query and compose services. However, the service discovery is done at design time by the scientists and the composition plan generation is also manual.

Static composition approaches have manual and labor-intensive task, and thus are not appropriate for large-scale web service composition endeavor.

#### Semi-dynamic composition approaches

This category is very broad. It includes all approaches that are neither static nor fully dynamic. citebrahim2003 presents a semi-dynamic service composition approach.

The approach requires a user to specify the request as high-level composition plan, which contains sequence of operations and control flows between operations. The concrete service binding is done at run-time. Thus, the approach relies on the composition plan created manually by the service requester.

[2] proposes a semi-dynamic model based composition approach. In this approach abstract level process model is generated manually in the form of computation independent model (CIM). Detailed process model is generated automatically using ontology, service registry and pre-existing database with lower level activity model. This approach requires domain knowledge to convert the CIM to executable composite service. The main difficulty with this approach is the requirement of domain knowledge and also someone has to do the initial high level composition plan manually.

[8] presents a semi-automatic composition techniques that allows users to select web services to add to the chain. They showed that automatic planner and human being can work together to generate the composite service that satisfy the user's request.

[46] proposed a template based semi-dynamic composition techniques. The approach uses templates to create a composition plan and binds concrete services at runtime.

In semi-dynamic composition approaches the process model generation labor is less than that of static approaches. However, it is still not flexible enough for large-scale web service composition.

**Dynamic composition approaches**

[14] presents an approach that utilizes a case-based reasoning machine learning method.

A case-based reasoning machine learning method is applied in the process of discovering and creating composite service. Service case-based, which are stored pre-assembled composite services, are used for the purpose of identifying relation-ships between services.

[6] propose a service composition technique using syntactic input/output matching. The approach does the candidate service discovery, and process model generation is done simultaneously using backward and forward chaining.

[7] presents a developer toolkit to form a composite service that uses entity-relation model to specify input/output parameters of the web services. To generate a composition plan a request should be given in the form of initial and final states. The composition plan is generated using rule-based chaining. The approach creates a local repository by re-defining existing services. The service re-definition is done in order to make the services understandable by the rule based planner. Mostly this approach is applicable to compose typical information web services, not services that constraints like account credit or debit or various business-business services.

[47] proposes a dynamic composition approach that uses SHOP2. SHOP2 is Hierarchical Task Network (HTN) planner. It starts from a general user request and decomposes the request into lower level sub-tasks. To decompose tasks or user request, it uses axioms, methods and operations created and stored using domain knowledge. In this approach composition plan is created by searching component services while planning . It uses rules to decompose the composite task step-by-step in order to find a task that can be accomplished using a single service. Though this approach does not need user intervention to generate composite service, creating the domain knowledge makes it less applicable.

Most of the attempts to achieve dynamic composition techniques uses AI planning techniques. For instance: Reiff-Marganiec[2008] proposes a composition approach that extend planning problem as model checking using semantics. Services are modeled as transition systems. S. Oh et al.(2007) also propose AI planning algorithm to compose services. They have used forward search(for service discovery) and regression search algorithm (to generate optimal sequence) that uses heuristics. D.Berardi, et al. [2008] modeled existing services as a finite state transition system. User request is given as transition system of target services. Then by traversing the FST system a composite service is generated. Service discovery and composition plan tasks are done automatically (simultaneously) .

[12][11] states that the way they perceive web service composition problem is determined by how services are represented. In their approach web services are conceived as an action and web service composition problem is perceived as planning problem. They adapt and extend Golog language to formally represent web services to enable automatic composition. Golog is a logic programming language built on top of the situation calculus. User request and constraints represented by first order language of situation calculus.

Thus, from discussions so far it can be seen that the complexity of creating the process model automatically is one of the main bottle necks to-wards achieving dynamic service composition.

In both forward and backward chaining cases the problem space is very large [9]. Some researchers try to combine forward and backward chaining in order to speedup the search process. For example [6] describes a technique to discover and compose web service using syntactical and semantical knowledge. In this work the starting point of the composition is the input and output of the user request. It has two ways, the first one is forward chaining mechanism that starts from the input of the request and discovers services by matching the inputs and then again try to find service which has the same input as the service output discovered in the first step (same input as user request). It repeats this step till it gets the output of the request or when the backward chain procedure gets a service input that matches the output of the service found by forward chain. The backward chaining starts from output of the user request and ends at the input or when it finds a matching service input from the discovered services in forward chain procedure. The two procedures run concurrently to speedup the service discovery process. After discovering all the necessary services another procedure performs the service composition task by linking a chain of services using one service output with input of the other service.

In AI planning approach composition problem is changed into planning problem in order to find the solution using various planning techniques. Normally, AI-planning problem is defined by a set of initial states, target states (the goal of the plan to be generated) and set of actions. The objective of planner will be to find a path or sequence of action that takes from the initial state to the target state by assuming that there is a knowledge about the set of all possible states of the world and set of actions. The main difference among AI planning methods used in service composition is the way the represent the knowledge and the usage of algorithms. These techniques work only when we have complete information about the existing services and their transition. Considering the fast growth of Web services, building a full knowledge base by converting all Web services into axioms will be expensive. Moreover, when the knowledge base description is direct map from existing web services the search space becomes big. That is why they mostly work in closed world assumption.

As a summary of all web service composition techniques explained above, Table 2.2 compares the different approaches with the following six comparison criteria.

1. PM generation: The way process model generation is performed (manual/ template-based/ automatic)

2. Domain knowledge: whether the approache uses domain knowledge or not (yes/no)

3. Simple/ complex PM : when the output process model by the composition approach includes only one control flow (sequential) it is categorized as simple PM, when the output PM includes two or more control flows ( out of sequential, alternative, concurrent ) it is categorized as complex PM;

4. Cycle in PM : whether the approach considers cyclic dependency or loop control flow

5. Closed world: whether the approach is applicable to a single domain or it works across any domains (yes/ no)

6. Semantic usage: whether the approach uses semantics or not (yes/ no)

Table 2.2 : Comparison table for composition techniques

| Year | Author | Approach | PM generation | Domain knowledge | Simple/ complex PM | Cycle in PM | Closed world | Semantic usage |
|---|---|---|---|---|---|---|---|---|
| 2004 | M.P. Papazoglou et al. | manual | no | yes | complex | yes | no | no |
| 2004 | Altintas et al., (Kepler) | manual | no | yes | complex | yes | no | no |
| 2003 | B.Medjahed, et al. | Sem-dynamic | no | yes | complex | NA | yes | yes |
| 2003 | Sivashanmugam et al. | Template based | no | yes | both | NA | no | no |
| 2006 | M. Fluegge et al. | Model based | no | yes | complex | NA | yes | Yes |
| 2003 | B.Limthanmaphon and Y. Zhang | Case base reasoning | yes | yes | complex | no | yes | yes |
| 2006 | Ramasamy, V. | chaining | yes | no | sequential | no | - | yes |
| 2002 | S.R. Ponnekanti and A.Fox | Planning | yes | yes | sequential | no | yes | no |
| 2004 | E. Sirin et al. | HTN | yes | yes | sequential | no | yes | no |
| 2007 | H. Meyer and M.Weske | Heuristic Search | yes | yes | complex | no | yes | no |
| 2007 | Seog-Chan O. et al | planning | yes | yes | sequential | no | yes | no |
| 2008 | D.Berardi | FSM | yes | yes | - | yes | yes | no |
| 2008 | H. Q. Yu and S. Reiff-Marganiec | Planning | yes | no | sequential | - | yes | no |
| 2009 | McIlraith et.al | Golog | yes | no | NA | - | yes | yes |
| 2009 | Y. Bo and Q. Zheng | graph plan | yes | yes | sequence | yes | yes | yes |

### 2.2.4 Summary on characteristics of static and dynamic composition techniques

Comparisons of static and dynamic composition techniques is given in table 2.3 below in a self explanatory way.

Table 2.3 : Comparison of static and dynamic composition techniques

| Criteria | Static | Dynamic |
|---|---|---|
| Process model generation time | Design/compile time | Run time(Late) |
| Service Discovery/selection time | Design/compile time | Run time |
| Service binding | Design/compile time (Early) i.e each instantiation of the composite service will be made up of the same constituent services. | Runtime(late) |
| Composition Design | compile time | Run time |
| Customization at run time | Not possible | Possible |
| Run time capability extension | Not possible | Possible |
| number of services provided | Limited | Not limited |
| Cost | Constant | Varies depending of the service selected |
| Fault tolerance and reliability | Less | High specifically in case a service becomes unavailable after some time which can be compensated by invocation of functionally equivalent service |
| Adaptability to changing environment | Less (eg. Old services are replaced by other ones inconsistence might be caused) | High (since service providers frequently leaving and joining ) |

# Chapter 3

# The proposed approach: automatic process model creation

This chapter describes the proposed approach. It starts by formulating the composite service problem. Following that, the adopted formalism for a web service, a user request and a composite service will be presented. Then, to facilitate easy understanding of the problem in focus and the proposed high level architecture description, a simple example will be given. A description of a more complex and complete example scenario that will be used throughout the thesis, in the explanation and illustration of the details of the proposed approach, will be given in chapter 4. Finally, a high level architecture that shows the proposed approach and its brief explanation at a conceptual level is illustrated with a simple example scenario. Further details of the proposed architecture are discussed in chapter 4, 5 and 6. The chapter is concluded by summarizing the proposed approach.

## 3.1 Problem formulation

A service composition process involves finding and combining services for a user request that can not be satisfied a single service. The partition of major tasks in service composition (these are process model creation, component abstract service (subtask) discovery and concrete service binding) could lead to different ways of understanding composition problem. While developing composition techniques, many researchers integrate one, two or all of the three subtasks of composition. For example, [22] perceives a service composition problem as the extended version of a matching problem. [48] proposes an approach which simultaneously does all the three major tasks of a service composition discussed above. A body of work by [6, 49, 50] provides composition techniques that combine the service discovery and the composition plan generation tasks. We believe that looking at each part of the composition subtask as a sub-problem of a service composition instead of considering them as a whole minimizes the complexity of a composition problem. As a result in this thesis a composition problem is seen as three problems that could potentially interrelate with each other, these are:

1. Task decomposition or component service description identification based on user request.
2. Creation of a process model for the identified subtask or an abstract service description.
3. Concrete service binding problem.

Based on this composition task division, a complete composition problem and a general solution approach is formulated as follows:

*Given a local repository with list of abstract service descriptions and a user request in which each abstract service description represents a collection of services (service community) that provide the same functionality, composite services that satisfy a user request could be created in three steps. First, using a goal-based match-making technique abstract service descriptions can be discovered to satisfy the goals of a user request. Then, the process model or composition plan should be generated in order to combine the component abstract services and form a composite service. Finally, the concrete service binding subtask should be done by selecting a service from members of the service community represented by abstract description and considering non-functional properties.*

The main focus of this thesis is on the second task, i.e., a process model creation. The other two problems are out of the scope of this thesis. Therefore, the process model generation sub-problem deals with:

"Given a list of component abstract service descriptions to be composed and a formal user request, how can it be possible to generate a process model or a composition plan for the composite service automatically? "

## 3.2 User request, abstract service and composite service specification

Extracting dependencies from the candidate services requires a suitable way of describing web services and user requests. Specifically our approach necessitates a formalization that has a functional abstract description of web services. Functional properties describe what the service exactly can do in the form of inputs, outputs, pre-conditions, and effects. These are used to perform the service discovery, matching and composition.

Although a user-request is in the form of a natural language, there are natural language processing techniques that parse a request and convert it into a formal description. This formal user request can be formulated as a web service. For our purpose, a similar description with OWL-S [32], both for web service and user request descriptions that includes a tuple (I, O, P, E, G) is taken. where:

- I: is the list of input parameters.
- O: is the list of output parameters.
- P: is the list of preconditions ( describing logical expressions that must be satisfied in order to invoke a (composite) service).
- E: is the list of effects (describing the changes to the current state resulting from the invocation of a (composite) service).
- G: is the list of goals.

## 3.3 Case study description

As a case study, an example of an e-health scenario that is partly taken from [25] is considered. This scenario assumes existing medical applications and devices interfaced by web services. By creating a composition of devices (a composition of devices wrapped as web services) one can enable an on-line patient follow-up, to reduce time-consuming consultations and medical checkups.

For this scenario, the following web services are considered: WS1 returns the blood pressure (BP) of a patient given the PatientID (PID) and DeviceAddress (ADD); WS2 returns the supervisor (Person) given a medical organization (Org) (Org is a general term for different departments); WS3 returns a Warning level (WL) given a blood pressure; WS4 returns the Emergency department(ED) given a level of Warning; WS5 returns the Organization (Org) given a Warning level. Table 3.1 shows the inputs and outputs of each service.

Table 3.1 : E-health scenario Input/Output description

| Web services | Inputs | Source web service | Outputs |
|---|---|---|---|
| WS1 | PID,ADD | User request | BP |
| WS2 | Org | WS5 | Person |
| WS3 | BP | WS1 | WL |
| WS4 | WL | WS3 | ED |
| WS5 | WL | WS3 | Org |

## 3.4 Architecture

This section provides an overview of the proposed general architecture followed by a brief description of each component of the architecture [51] using the example scenario.

### 3.4.1 Candidate abstract service description selection

Figure 3.1 shows the proposed three layered general architecture. The first layer consists of a data repository, an incoming user request and a service matching module. The data repository contains a statically available list of abstract semantic service descriptions in a specified format as discussed in section 3.2. The abstract service description is a description of a group of services, which are sometimes called a service community, with an equivalent functionality. In otherwords, an abstract descripton is a single functional description for all functionally equivalent available services in a repository, regardless of their quality(non functional property). A user is expected to describe his or her request in terms of goals, inputs and outputs to facilitate candidate service discovery. Thus candidate abstract services will be discovered from the local repository using a goal based discovery mechanism based on a user requirement. For the e-health scenario, the services described in section 3.3 are assumed to be candidate services discovered by the matching module (see the architecture in figure 3.1) which has a goal based discovery mechanism. Table 3.1 gives the input/output descriptions of the candidate abstract services; the third column of the table shows from where a service gets its inputs. This description is given here to clearly show the dependency generation process which is the bottomline for the full composition steps. Otherwise, the research doesnt́ deal with the abstract service discovery mechanisms and this thesis does not further discuss it.

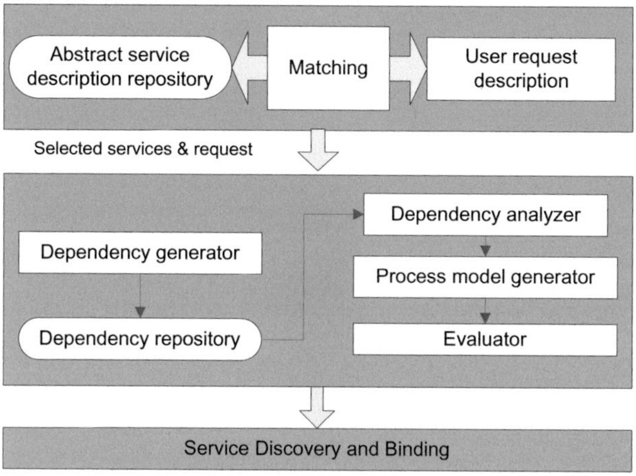


Figure 3.1 : Architecture

The second layer, which is the core part of this thesis, consists of a data repository and six modules which are responsible for creating the process model using the output of the first layer. The dependency repository contains service dependencies occurring during composition. The role of each module in this layer is described as follows:

### 3.4.2 Service dependency generator

Although service descriptions are expected to include semantic annotations to facilitate the dependency extraction process, dependencies are not expected to be included in such descriptions. This is because, firstly, it requires prior knowledge about composition requirements of services at design time and this limits flexibility. Secondly, a service could have different types of dependencies for different composition requests.

This means, achieving a comprehensive prior knowledge of dependencies is unlikely. Therefore, incorporating semantic dependency description in a service description is unpractical. We proposed an architecture that has an automatic dependency generator module.

The module extracts service dependencies upon receiving a formal description of the user request and a list of semantic service descriptions. The dependency extraction is based on two inputs received from layer one; these are semantic description of abstract services and a user request with an additional annotation that enables the dependency generator to extract different dependencies. The extracted dependencies will be represented in an appropriate data structure and will be stored in the dependency repository ready for a further use or re-use when needed. For example, for the e-health scenario, $WS_2$ is dependent on $WS_5$. Such dependencies among services and other dependencies between services and a user request can be found by using IOPE matching with a support of semantic descriptions.

### Service dependency representation

Dependency can be represented as a graph or equivalently as an adjacency matrix. For example [39], [41], [40], [22], [21] and [20] use a graph to represent dependency. [42] and [16] represent dependencies as a matrix.

Most of the approaches in the related work agree on the general representation of service dependency, i.e. the representation of semantics is more or less the same, except for a slight difference in the detail(syntax). For example, some construct service dependency graph(SDG) as a directed graph with service nodes and dependency edges, and others represent with parameter (data) nodes and service edges. Such kind of a difference is only a syntactic difference that result while trying to fit the specific application area or the proposed algorithm. There is also no global agreement in syntax for dependency representation either as a graph or a matrix.

In this thesis, a directed graph and an adjacency matrix are used to represent I/O dependencies among services. The reason why both representations are used is due to the existence of advantages and disadvantages in both approaches. For instance, for a very dense dependency, a matrix model is more appropriate than a graph in terms of space complexity. Moreover, the representation has significant influence on the computational complexity of the algorithm in use. If, for example the algorithm has an adjacent node search operation, with matrix representation, a single adjacent node search takes only one value check. It could take O(E)(where E=Edges) operation in case of a graph. On the other hand, if the algorithm requires the checking of neighboring nodes, a matrix representation takes O(n)(where n=number os nodes); this will be O(E) operations for a graph representation. Thus, based on the application dominant feature different representation can be used.

A matrix that models a dependency is a square matrix $(nxn)$ where $n$ equals the number of available services to form the composite service. Each row and column represents a candidate web service $((WS_i))$ for the composition. Let a composite service requires $n$ web services: $WS1, WS2, ...WSn$. Then the dependency matrix (DM) is defined as:

$$\text{DM=} \begin{bmatrix} C_{11} & \cdots & C_{1n} \\ \vdots & \ddots & \vdots \\ C_{n1} & \cdots & C_{nn} \end{bmatrix} whereC_{ij} = \begin{cases} 1, & \text{if WSi is dependent on WSj} \\ 0, & \text{if otherwise} \end{cases}$$

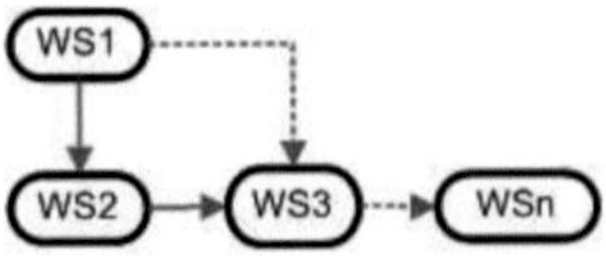


Figure 3.2 : Dependency representation using directed graph

If a service on the $i_{th}$ column is dependent on a service on the $j_{th}$ row, then the $C_{ij}$ value of the matrix will be 1, otherwise, it will be zero.

A directed graph, which can be equivalently represented by an adjacency matrix, can also be used to represent dependencies between services. Let a directed graph that models dependency has $n$ nodes, where $n$ equals to the available services to form the composite service and edges of the graph represent the dependency link. The edge direction indicates the service dependency flow. For instance, if the $i^{th}$ service is dependent on the $j^{th}$ service then there will be a directed edge from $S_i$ to $S_j$, where $S_i$ and $S_j$ are represented by nodes.

### 3.4.3 Extracting cyclic dependency

The dependency graph or matrix shows either unidirectional or bidirectional communication between services. In a unidirectional communication, one service gives its outputs and the other receives.them. As a result there will be a one way dependency between a service input provider and receiver. When all dependencies are unidirectional, the dependency graph will also be direct acyclic graph. In cases of a bidirectional communication, a service starts execution and gives a partial output to another service and waits for a reply to finish an execution. Or sometimes service(s) might need more than one invocation to accomplish a task. In such cases, the dependency graph or matrix will include a cyclic dependency. However, in case of the existence of cycles, most of the existing approaches that use dependency graph and/or matrix for various applications face difficulty, because their basic assumption is the non-existence of a cyclic dependency. As a result, finding and extracting a cyclic dependency is compulsory for any approach that uses a service dependency. In this research, we propose a method for extracting cyclic dependencies and regeneration of an acyclic dependency graph/ or matrix as a first step in generation of composition plan [52].

A cyclic dependency extraction takes place in both proposed approaches. In the matrix based approach a power matrix based algorithm is used to extract the cyclic dependency. In section 5.2 a detail explanation can be found. In the graph based approach the Tarjan algorithm [53] is used which is originally proposed to find strongly connected components in a directed graph. The algorithm can also enumerates all cycles by taking the directed dependency graph in the form of an adjacency list. By considering each cyclic component subgraph as a compound node, a new acyclic graph is generated. In section 6.3 a detail explanation of the Tarjan algorithm and its implementation is given in chapter 7.

### 3.4.4 Dependency analyzer

This module takes the service dependencies stored by the dependency generator as an input and it analyzes them to put them in an understandable and interpretable format. The analyzer has a key role in processing and converting raw dependency data into data that are more applicable. Anticipated application areas are alternative process model generation, development of process adaptability or composite service management. The approach proposed in this thesis analyzes a dependency by counting the number of services dependent on it (N1), number of services a service is dependent on (N2) and the dependency between a service and a user request(s), which provide the priority level of a service.

When the dependency represented in matrix form N1 is found by adding the columns of the full dependency matrix(direct and indirect). Similarly N2 is found by adding the rows of the full dependency matrix. In case of a graph, they can be found by counting incoming and outgoing edges. For the example scenario considered here $WS_1$ has higher execution priority because it takes inputs directly from the user request. But $WS_5$ has the least priority since $WS_5$ takes inputs from $WS_3$ and $WS_3$ takes inputs from $WS_1$. This shows $WS_5$ is dependent on two services, $WS_3$ and $WS_1$.

### 3.4.5 Process model generator

A process model, that will be generated 'by the proposed approach, gives services invocation orders based on the data dependency. It provides core constituents of a composite service which is given by a composite service structure description. Nevertheless, it needs an additional enhancement before final deployment. For instance, inclusion of data transformations, mapping, translation and transactions.

The composite service structure description holds information about service components and how they interconnect with each other. This includes possible control flows that form the process model. Both structural and behavioral relationships among the component services of a composite service can be determined from their dependency.

As discussed before, the dependency extraction among the component services is vital for this step, and it can be supported by the semantic description of services. The possible control flows that form the process model are sequential, alternative, concurrent and iterative. Thus, by taking the analyzer outputs, the process model generator will further interpret and associate it with any of the control flows. By doing so, the process model generator tries to create possible process models for the intended composite service. For the e-health this sequential process model found by simply sorting based on the number of services a particular service dependent on : $WS_1 \Rightarrow WS_3 \Rightarrow WS_5 \Rightarrow WS_2 \Rightarrow WS_4$.

In case of a graph representation, the execution plan is generated using a topological sorting algorithm. A topological sorting is often used in scheduling jobs or tasks given precedence constraints. In our case, the precedence constraint is the dependency graph. It takes an acyclic graph and outputs linear ordering tasks (nodes/services). We adopt the modified topological sorting that is used to sort threads that can be executed concurrently [54](see algorithm 8 in chapter 6). The composition plan generated by this algorithm for the travel scenario is given in figure 3.3.

In the proposed architecture, the dependency analyzer is coupled with the process model generator, so that they work interactively and iteratively.

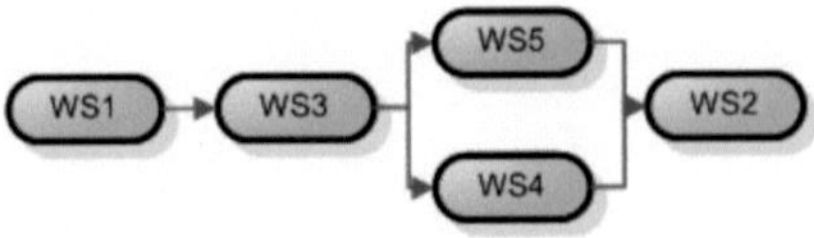


Figure 3.3 : Process model

### 3.4.6 Validator/Evaluator

The validator is responsible for checking the correctness of the generated process model(s) based on a temporal or an execution order. If the generated process model does not fully or partially satisfy the dependency pre-requiste then it should be excluded.

The evaluator is responsible to evaluate and compare the generated process models.

## 3.5 Chapter summary and conclusions

Dependencies reflect the potential of a service to affect or be affected by the elements of other services that compose the application. Analysing and tracking of dependencies is important in SOA management. However, little attention is given to it so far to-wards the usage of a service dependency in an automatic service composition. In this thesis, we argue that a semantic description of web services and user request enables detection of dependencies between services automatically. This in turn allows the automatic creation of composite services. We believe that the proposed architecture will enable to consider a service composition as a service dependency identification and analysis problem. This opening ways for developing more flexible and scalable applications from smaller, semantically described services.

# Chapter 4

# Automatic service dependency extraction

As mentioned in section 1.2 the main focus of this thesis is on establishing automatic process model creation methods based on an automatic extraction of dependency among web services. In this chapter, details of the automatic dependency extraction process and the description of an example scenario will be presented. The example scenario described in section 4.1 will be used throughout the thesis for illustrating the proposed methodologies.

## 4.1 Description of example scenario

To demonstrate the applicability of the proposed methodologies an on-line shopping scenario is considered. For the sake of clarity the real life scenario is slightly modified, without losing its main features, so that it can effectively demonstrate the proposed approaches step by step.

In an on-line shopping consumers typically browse through an on-line catalog to view the products offered for sale, purchase the products based on their preferences and get them delivered. To accomplish these sub-tasks from viewing the product detail to receiving the product at their gate, the following specific tasks shall be executed:

- displaying products information,

- checking availability of the product requested by a user,
- offering different shipping methods (express or normal) and determine a delivery date based on the weather forecast,
- insuring the product,
- calculating the total price based on the tax amount, the insurance charge and the delivery cost,
- locating the user (identifying location of a user from IP or based on information obtained from completed address form),
- show the total price for the user in his local currency, and
- verifying payment information.

Table 4.1 shows the input and output description of 12 web services that are presumed as requirements to accomplish an on-line shopping.

Table 4.1 : On-line shopping scenario study Input/Output description

| | WS name | Inputs | Source WS | Outputs |
|---|---|---|---|---|
| WS1 | OnlineCatalog | Item selection | UR | Item detail={<br>Item category<br>Item code<br>Item quantity<br>Item Price<br>Item value}<br>IP address |
| WS2 | CustomerLocator | IP address | WS1 | Customer location |
| WS3 | ItemChecker | Item category<br>Item code<br>Item quantity<br>Number of Item | WS1<br><br><br>WS3 | Availability<br>Number of Items |
| WS4 | TaxCalculator | Item category<br>Item Price | WS1 | Tax amount |
| WS5 | Insurance | Item category<br>Item quantity<br>Item Price<br>Item value | WS1 | Insurance reference<br>Insurance cost |
| WS6 | GetItem | Availability | WS3 | Location |
| WS7 | PriceCalculator | Item price<br>Tax amount<br>Insurance cost<br>Delivery cost | WS1<br>WS4<br>WS5<br>WS10 | Total price |
| WS8 | POC | Item detail<br>Total price in local currency | WS1<br>WS12 | Purchase order |
| WS9 | WeatherForecast | Item location<br>Customer location | WS6<br>WS2 | Weather |
| WS10 | Delivery | Weather<br>Item detail<br>Receipt (payment confirmation) | WS9<br>WS1<br>WS11 | Delivery cost<br>Delivery order<br>Tracking number |
| WS11 | Payment | Purchase Order | WS8 | Receipt |
| WS12 | Currency converter | Total price | WS7 | Total price in local currency |

To observe the logical execution order of individual web services in a composition, the scenario is analyzed and data-flow diagram is created manually. Figure 4.1 shows the manually generated data-flow of the on-line shopping scenario. This provides a benchmark to cross check the correctness of the process models generated by the proposed approaches. It also provides a perspective on the stepwise execution of tasks in order to accomplish a requested task.

The web services involved are explained as follows:

1. A user browses the on-line catalog service (WS1) to choose items he/she wants to buy. This service provides the user with data on item details and it serves as interface to receive the input from the user. When the user selects an item, the on-line catalog service outputs information about the details of the selected item (Item category, Item code, Item price, item value, and quantity). Also the catalog takes preliminary customer information (mainly customer IP address).

2. The Customer locator (WS2) gets the IP address from the catalog service and outputs customer location. It prompts the user to change or edit customer location information as required.

3. The tax Calculator (WS4) takes the item name, category and price from the on-line Catalog service and calculates tax and provides information about the tax amount to the total price calculator.

4. The item availability checker (WS3) inputs item details provided by the catalog service in step one and checks the availability of the selected items in stock at the required quantity. This service first counts the number of items requested and checks the availability of all items. Based on this count value it may

execute more than once (self loop) when more than one item is selected. It also checks the availability of the selected item(s) first in a stock. If the item is not available in the stock then it checks the availability of this item with other vendors or manufacturers. If the requested item is found then it sends confirmation otherwise, in case the item is not available neither in the stock nor with other vendors or manufacturer, it ends the process.

5. The insurance service (WS5) calculates insurance cost by taking an item code, name and price from the catalog service. Then outputs an insurance cost and an insurance number.

6. The get item service (WS6) returns the item location by taking the item availability from the item availability checker.

7. The price calculator service (WS7) returns the total price given an item's basic price, an insurance cost, a tax and a delivery cost.

8. The weather forecast (WS9) service gets a customer location from the customer locator, an item location from the get item service and outputs the weather forecast at the item and customer location.

9. The currency converter (WS12) returns the total price in local currency as well as in Euros by taking a customer location and a total price.

10. The delivery service (WS10) gets information on an item category (from catalog), an item location (from get item), a customer location(from customer locator), and weather both at customer and item location (from weather forecast) and then returns the delivery cost to the total price calculator. It then

waits for the payment confirmation before returning the delivery order and the tracking number for the end user.

11. The purchase order creator POC (WS8) gets basic inputs from the catalog service and the total price from the currency converter and generates the Purchase Order (PO) for the selected items and sends the PO to the payment service.

12. The payment service (WS11) takes PO from POC and it provides alternative payment methods (pay pal or credit card) to a user. When the payment is made it sends the payment confirmation receipt to the end user and the delivery service. When the payment confirmation reaches the delivery service, it gives delivery order and returns the tracking number to the end user. Here, it should be noted that there is a bi-directional communication(cycle) among the delivery and the payment service.

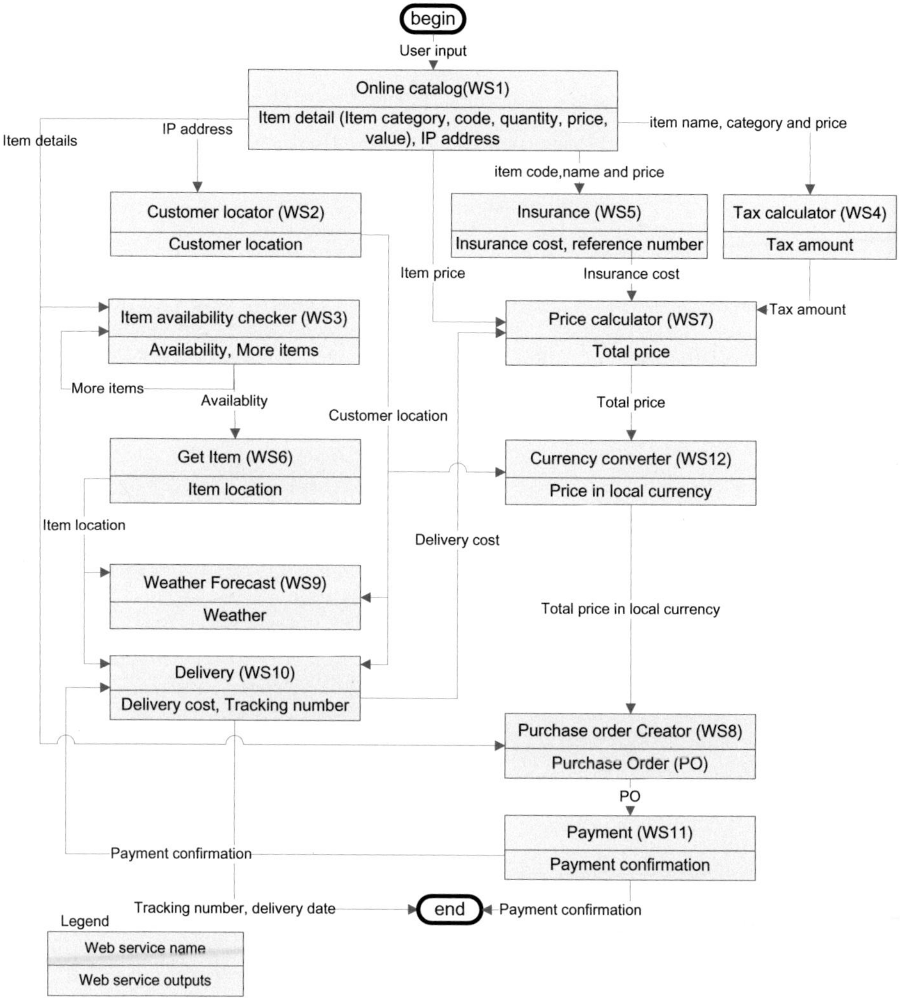


Figure 4.1 : Data flow diagram

## 4.2 Service dependency identification

The establishment of a composite services based application necessitates interaction, and data exchange among individual component services. This leads to the emergence of different types of dependencies among the services involved in the composition, such as:

1. Input/Output (I/O) dependency: this occurs when a service requires or provides data from/to another service. For example, in the on-line shopping scenario since WS2 (customer locator) gets its input from WS1 (on-line catalog), WS2 has I/O dependency on WS1.

2. Constraint dependency: this occurs due to user constraints. For example, based on a user choice the insurance cost could be added or escaped.

3. Cause and effect dependency: this occurs when a service has preconditions to be satisfied based on the effects of other services. For example, the delivery service needs the completion of a payment service before it sends the delivery confirmation (tracking number).

Such dependencies between two services could occur directly, which we call a direct dependency or it might occur indirectly through (an) intermediate service(s), which we call indirect dependency. Service dependency can also occur in an explicit or an implicit manner. Explicit direct I/O dependencies among services occur when a service requires/or provides data from/to another service. An explicit dependency can be readily visible and extractable from service descriptions. On the other hand an implicit dependency can not be directly expressed in service descriptions. In this thesis, we used direct dependency and explicit direct dependency interchangeably.

Generally, managing dependencies is considered to be the basis for defining task (service) coordination mechanisms [55]. Sequential, alternative, iterative and concurrent coordination mechanisms are the basic coordination mechanism in any business process or dependency management. These coordination mechanisms are used during process model creation for the composite services.

The two proposed approaches start with automatic extraction of I/O dependencies among candidate abstract services for the composition. The first approach, i.e. dependency matrix based approach (chapter 5), utilizes a two stepped I/O dependencies extraction procedure. The dependencies are represented using a matrix. The first step is the extraction of direct I/O dependency and storing it in a matrix (Direct Dependency Matrix(DDM)). The second is extraction of indirect dependency and storing it in a matrix(Indirect Dependency Matrix (IDM)) from the DDM. Then summing up the two dependency matrices provides the full I/O dependency matrix (Full Dependency Matrix (FDM)). The other alternative way is directly extracting full dependency from direct dependency. The issue of service dependency representation using matrix is discussed in section 3.4.2.

The second approach, i.e. dependency graph based approach (chapter 6), uses only the explicit direct dependency. It represents the dependency using a directed graph (see chapter 3.4.2 ).

### 4.2.1 Explicit direct Input/Output dependency extraction

An explicit direct I/O dependency between two services exists if at least one output of a service is taken as an input by the other service. During a service composition, all inputs of web services are either from a user request or from another web service. For the purpose of explaining the proposed approach we used an example that has almost perfect match between I/O parameters described in section 4.1. However, in real case scenario it is not possible to get services whose interface shows a perfect match. In our approach we use the concept of finding semantic similarity between service inputs and outputs. Thus, the extraction of explicit direct I/O dependency is done using semantically enabled I/O matching technique, which is adopted from [35]. It uses the following three semantic I/O matching functions proposed in [35] and intersection of I/O parameter sets proposed in [36]:

1. Exact I/O matching function: this matching occurs when the output parameter of one web service (say WS1) and the input parameter of another web service (say WS2) are equivalent concepts, where WS1 and WS2 are services whose dependency is being assessed.

2. Plug in function: this matching occurs when output of WS1 is sub-concept of input WS2; for example, if WS2 (customer locator) of the on-line shopping scenario outputs full address of the customer that includes (city name, zip code, telephone etc) and WS9 (weather forecast ) might require only the city name. The input of WS9 is a sub-concept of the output of WS2.

3. Intersection: this occurs when the intersection of the output of WS1 and the input WS2 is satisfiable. For example, from the on-line scenario

$$Input(GetItem) \bigcap Output(onlinecatalog) = \{(Itemcategory, Itemcode, Itemquantity\}$$

4. Fail : if all the above conditions are not satisfied.

Figure 4.2 schematizes the dependency matrix extraction process which is the detailed version of the first module of the second layer of the general architecture presented in chapter 3 (figure 3.1).

The dependency generator checks the intersection between the whole set of input parameters of one service with the whole set of output parameters of the other service. To do the intersection operation each input parameter should be checked with the output parameter using exact or plug in function. i.e. $In(WS1) \bigcap Out(WS2) \neq \phi$, If and only if at least one pair of parameter sets (each from Input (WS1) and Output (WS2)) has either exact or plug-in relationship, then there is dependency between the two services. This check is done because the main aim is to find out from which services a particular service gets its inputs, i.e. on which services it is dependent on.

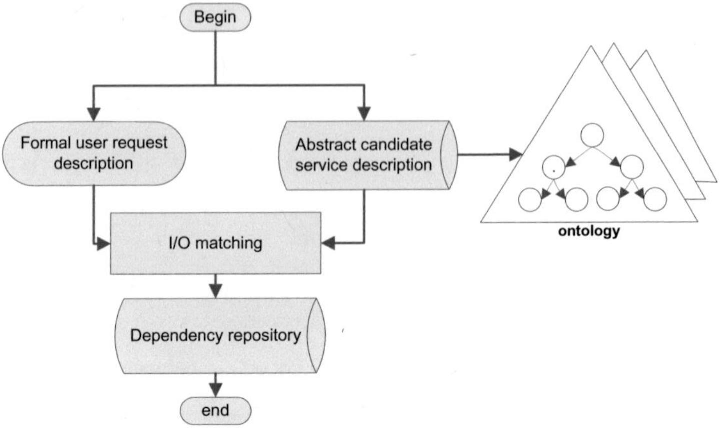


Figure 4.2 : Dependency matrix extraction

By applying this function the explicit direct dependency of the on-line shopping example scenario is extracted. This extracted service dependency can be represented as a matrix or a graph. Mapping from a graph to a matrix and from a matrix to a graph is possible. Therefore, if the matrix is available, the corresponding graph can be drawn or vice-versa. So, without loss of generality, here it is decided to store the dependency among component services of the scenario in the form of a matrix. Matrix 5.1 shows the explicit direct input/output dependencies for the scenario described in section 4.1. The dependency graph can be drawn directly from the dependency matrix when required.

**Matrix 4.1** Direct dependency matrix for on-line shopping scenario

$DDM =$

| | $WS1$ | $WS2$ | $WS3$ | $WS4$ | $WS5$ | $WS6$ | $WS7$ | $WS8$ | $WS9$ | $WS10$ | $WS11$ | $WS12$ |
|---|---|---|---|---|---|---|---|---|---|---|---|---|
| $WS1$ | 0 | 0 | 0 | 0 | 0 | 0 | 0 | 0 | 0 | 0 | 0 | 0 |
| $WS2$ | 1 | 0 | 0 | 0 | 0 | 0 | 0 | 0 | 0 | 0 | 0 | 0 |
| $WS3$ | 1 | 0 | 1 | 0 | 0 | 0 | 0 | 0 | 0 | 0 | 0 | 0 |
| $WS4$ | 1 | 0 | 0 | 0 | 0 | 0 | 0 | 0 | 0 | 0 | 0 | 0 |
| $WS5$ | 1 | 0 | 0 | 0 | 0 | 0 | 0 | 0 | 0 | 0 | 0 | 0 |
| $WS6$ | 0 | 0 | 1 | 0 | 0 | 0 | 0 | 0 | 0 | 0 | 0 | 0 |
| $WS7$ | 1 | 0 | 0 | 1 | 1 | 0 | 0 | 0 | 0 | 1 | 0 | 0 |
| $WS8$ | 1 | 0 | 0 | 0 | 0 | 0 | 1 | 0 | 0 | 0 | 0 | 1 |
| $WS9$ | 0 | 1 | 0 | 0 | 0 | 1 | 0 | 0 | 0 | 0 | 0 | 0 |
| $WS10$ | 1 | 0 | 0 | 0 | 0 | 0 | 0 | 0 | 1 | 0 | 1 | 0 |
| $WS11$ | 0 | 0 | 0 | 0 | 0 | 0 | 0 | 1 | 0 | 0 | 0 | 0 |
| $WS12$ | 0 | 0 | 0 | 0 | 0 | 0 | 1 | 0 | 0 | 0 | 0 | 0 |

### 4.2.2 Indirect service dependency identification

Since dependency holds transitivity property one can extract an indirect I/O dependencies between services from a direct I/O dependency. For example, if service B has a direct dependency on service A and service C has a direct dependency on service B then service C will have indirect dependency on service A. Thus, one should traverse all possible explicit direct service dependency chains to extract explicit indirect dependencies. This dependency chain is a linked list of services that starts from a service in focus and terminates with a service that does not have an explicit direct dependency with any service. The link between individual services in a chain represents the explicit direct dependency between services.

Thus, an explicit indirect I/O dependency exists if and only if:

- a service has explicit direct dependency to at least one service,
- there exists service in a chain of explicit direct dependencies that does not have an explicit direct dependency with a particular service in focus. For example, one possible direct dependency chain of WS8 from on-line shopping scenario is : $WS8 \Rightarrow WS7 \Rightarrow WS4 \Rightarrow WS1 \Rightarrow none$. From this chain, since WS8 also has an explicit direct dependency with WS1, only an indirect dependency with WS4 is counted. When representing indirect dependency all direct dependencies should be excluded to control redundant counting of dependency.

The actual extraction of indirect dependency is done in two ways and the efficient method is implemented. As a first attempt, the following algorithm is developed based on a transitive closure property of dependency to generate the explicit indirect dependency matrix from an explicit direct dependency matrix. It takes explicit direct dependency matrix as input and returns an explicit indirect dependency matrix.

**Algorithm 1** Indirect dependency extraction main function caller

INPUT : Direct Dependency Matrix (DDM)

$n = number\ of\ services$

$i = 1$

**while** i<=n **do**

  $Function(i, i)$

  $i = i + 1$

**end while**

**Algorithm 2** The recursive function of indirect dependency extraction

```
Function(k, m)
n = number of services
for j = 0 to n − 1 do
    if DDM[j][k] = 1 then
        if DDM[j][m]! = 1 then
            IDM[j][m]=1
            Function(j,m)
        end if
    end if
    return 0
end for
```

Algorithm 1 refers to the call of the main recursive function in algorithm 2 for each service in order to get all services a service has indirect dependency. In line 4 of algorithm 1, the while loop shows the iterative call of an indirect dependency extractor function for each service ($n$ services). Two arguments are passed while calling the recursive function. The first parameter stands for the last service in the services dependency chain and the second one is for the service in which the search for indirect dependency is being made. For one function call the recursive function tries to get all possible dependency chains by making recursive calls. During the recursive calls (till the recursive function returns the control to the caller) the second argument will not be changed. This is because the argument is associated to the service for which the caller is looking for indirect dependencies.

Algorithm 2 describes the recursive function that looks for chains of services to get the indirect dependencies. This recursive function has two parameters. As mentioned before the first parameter corresponds to the service in focus and the second corresponds to the last service in the service dependency chain. In line 3, 4 and 5 of this algorithm the dependency chains will be explored and an indirect dependency matrix value will be assigned. The value checking at line 4 is done to exclude direct dependencies inside an indirect dependency matrix. All direct dependencies should be excluded to avoid redundancy. For example, for the on-line shopping scenario the following chain of dependencies exists:

1. $WS1 \Rightarrow none$ ; Since WS1 has no direct dependency to any service it doesn't have a chain of service dependencies which shows indirect dependency.

2. $WS7 \Rightarrow WS1 \Rightarrow none$; One possible service chain with only one direct dependency.

   $WS7 \Rightarrow WS4 \Rightarrow WS3 \Rightarrow WS1 \Rightarrow none$; in this chain there are 4 services. The service in focus is WS7 that has direct dependency to WS4 and WS1 and indirect dependency to WS3.

As a second attempt, the Warshall algorithm is used to find the transitive closure of dependencies which generates a complete dependency matrix from explicit direct dependency matrix. It takes explicit direct dependency matrix as input and returns an full dependency matrix.

**Algorithm 3** Warshall algorithm: indirect dependency extraction

```
1: Input : AdjacencymatrixDDMofnelements
2: Output : AdjacencymatrixFullDMofnelements
3: FullDM := DDM[initializeFullDMtoDDM]
4: for i = 0 to n do
5:     for j = 0 to n do
6:         if DDM[i][j] = 1 then
7:             for k = 0 to n do
8:                 if DDM[j][k] == 1 then
9:                     FullDM[i][k]=1
10:                end if
11:            end for
12:        end if
13:    end for
14: end for
15: End of Warshall
```

Algorithm 3 describes the Warshall transitive closure algorithm that looks for chains of services to get indirect dependencies. In line 6 this algorithm explores the dependency chains and in line 8 the full dependency matrix value is assigned.

Both the above methods can be used to get the complete dependency matrix, which is a combination of direct and indirect dependency, extracted from its direct dependency matrix. But, both ways of the indirect dependency extractor algorithm work when there is no cyclic dependency, otherwise it will enter into an infinite loop and results in a stack overflow error. Therefore, cyclic dependency shall be identified and extracted prior to indirect dependency extraction. It is found convenient to discuss method for extracting cyclic dependency from matrix in section 5.2. The indirect dependency extraction process description will continue in section 5.3.

Two equally valid process models can be created based on two calculated numbers N1 and N2 above.

## 4.3 Chapter summary and discussion

This chapter provides the dependency extraction procedure which is based on semantic description of web services and semantic enabled I/O matching techniques. This step is crucial for the two proposed methods of process model generation that are presented in the next two chapters. Both methods rely on the dependency extraction method presented here. Figure 4.3 shows the general structure of the full methodology of this thesis. It shows the input, expected output of the methodology and the role of dependency extractor for the matrix based and the graph based approach.

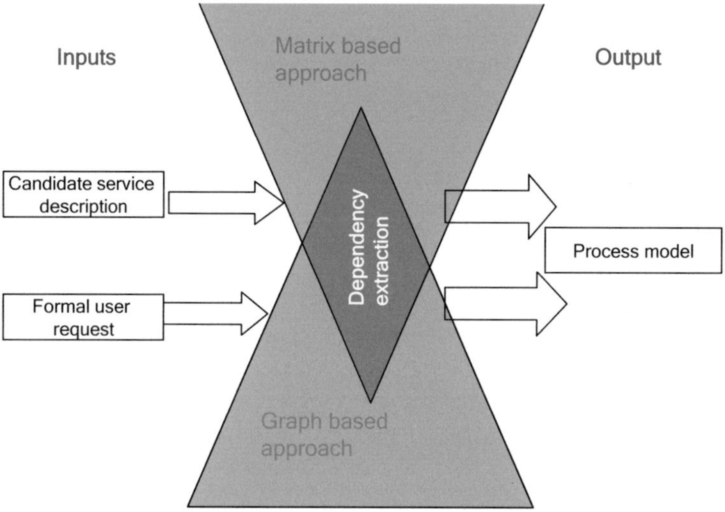


Figure 4.3 : General approach structure

Since the dependency extraction process does one by one I/O matching, its complexity in the worst case scenario is O (#(Input parameters) #(Output parameters)). The first indirect dependency generator does recursive calls that vary with the direct dependency in concern which makes the calculation of complexity difficult. Thus, this will be checked during experimental evaluation. But the second way of indirect dependency extraction is a known algorithm and its theoretical complexity is $O(n^3)$(where n is number of services).

The dependency considered in this thesis is only the I/O dependency aspect which has a major contribution for composition plan generation. Unlike all other methods that construct dependency between all services in repository we generated dependency between candidate services automatically. We believe, pre-computing all possible semantic links (dependency) between services might lead to extended graph that increases the complexity of plan creation. To generate composition plan the majority dependency based composition techniques often used graph traverse algorithms, this arose O(number of vertex * number of edge), which is fully dependent on the number of edges and vertices that in turn is dependent on the number of services in the repository(even services with same functionality). Therefore, compared to the quadratic complexity of our approach this complexity is much bigger when the number of services in repository increases. To tackle such complexity problem in existing approaches, our approach assumes goal based candidate service discovery upon receipt of user request. This approach takes those discovered candidate services, extracts their dependency, analyzes it and then generates the composition plan.

Contrary to other proposed approaches our method explicitly shows which service is dependent on which service in its dependency model. For example: casual link matrix only shows the degree of similarity between Input and output parameters, graph based composition techniques proposed by [22] shows the dependency between services implicitly but the dependency graph is generated at design time.

# Chapter 5

# Matrix based automatic process model generation

This chapter presents the proposed matrix based automatic process model generation approach [56]. This approach, first extracts direct dependencies from candidate abstract service description. Then it automatically extracts existing indirect dependencies from the direct dependency extracted earlier. For extracting indirect dependencies the approach uses two alternative algorithms that is based on the transitive closure property.

The approach uses a matrix to model the dependencies among web services. The matrix values are either 1 or 0 depending on existence and non existence of dependency, i.e. if a service on $i_{th}$ column is dependent on a service on $j_{th}$ row then the $C_{ij}$ value of the matrix will be 1 otherwise it will be zero. This matrix representation facilitates a simplistic mathematical dependency analysis for generating important indicators during the automatic process model creation. The process model is generated using a sorting algorithm that uses the dependency matrix analysis result found from dependency matrix as a sorting criteria.

First, a stepwise description of dependency matrix based automatic process model generation is provided. Following that, a detailed explanation of each step of the PM creation, with the help of example scenario, is presented. Finally, a summary of this technique, advantages and its shortcomings are presented.

## 5.1 Automatic process model generation procedure

The detailed architecture of the proposed dependency matrix based approach is provided in figure 5.1. This approach uses two sets of information for automatic creation of process model:

1. Direct dependencies among abstract candidate services,
2. A formal user request description.

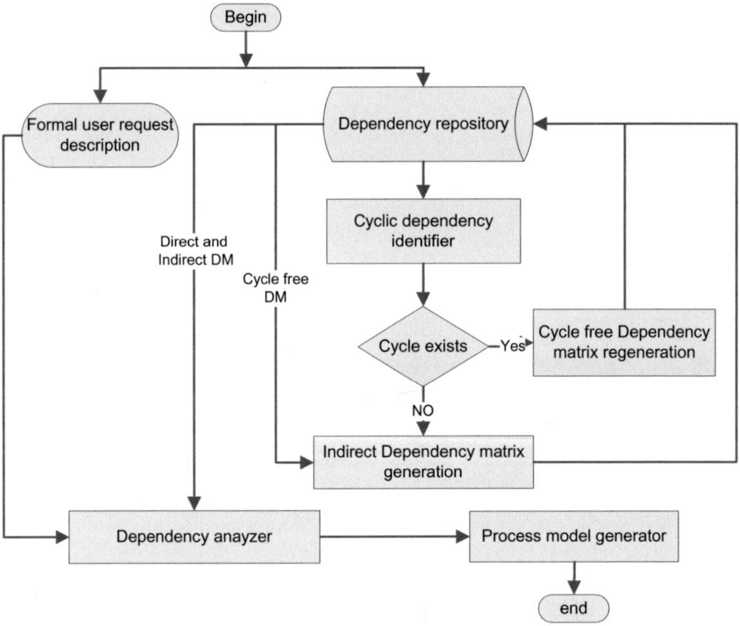


Figure 5.1 : Dependency matrix based approach architecture

The steps for automatic PM generation are summarized as follows:

1. Construct direct I/O dependency matrix (DDM). (section 4.2.1)

2. Identify cyclic dependencies from a direct dependency matrix by computing a power of matrix and then construct a cycle free direct I/O dependency matrix.

3. Identify an indirect I/O dependencies by recursively exploring the cycle free direct dependencies and construct the indirect dependency matrix (IDM).

4. Merge the cycle free direct and the indirect dependencies and form one dependency matrix (we call this Full dependency matrix (FDM)). Alternatively construct the full dependency matrix from DDM in one step using the Warshall algorithm, in this case step 3 should be skipped.

5. Calculate the number of services that depend on a particular service $WS_j$ by adding respective values in the column j from a matrix found in step 4. We call this number N1.

6. Calculate the number of services providing input to a particular service (say $WS_i$) by adding the row i values of DDM found in step 4. We call this number N2.

7. Use simple sorting algorithm to generate a process model by sorting services based on calculated values in step 5 and step 6 .

This is a simplified stepwise description of the process model generation architecture schematized in figure 5.1. The detailed explanation on automatic explicit direct and indirect dependency extraction procedure (step 1 and 3 of the PM generation process above) is given in chapter 4. The other steps of the approach listed above are further explained in the following successive sections.

## 5.2 Extracting cyclic dependency

As it is introduced in chapter 3 , cyclic dependency occurs when there is bidirectional communication between services. Cycles in service dependency are indicators of an iterative control flow among services participating in a cycle existing with in a process model. Therefore, extracting the cyclic dependency is apparently among the major steps of an automatic process model generation.

We have extensively explored a matrix properties with an intent of finding a property that could indicate existence of cycles. From this exploration the following matrix properties are found as indicators of a cyclic dependency, i.e. a cyclic dependency exists when one of the following conditions are satisfied:

1. When a diagonal element of dependency matrix is 1. This implies a service is dependent on itself. It also means only one service is involved in the cycle which forms a self loop in the resulting process model. If more than one diagonal elements of a matrix have a value of 1, then this indicates existence of more than one self loop(cycle) in the process model. Symbolically, let $i$ represent row number, and j represent column number. For i=j if DDM[i, j]=1, then service $i$ is dependent on itself. Self-loops practical interpretation is, a service needs to execute more than once to accomplish the composite task. As a result a loop control flow should be attached to it. For example, the on-line shopping scenario DDM (matrix 5.1) has value 1 on WS3(Item checker). This is because

WS3 needs to run a number of times to check the availability of all items requested by the user. Such as, if a consumer chooses n different items then WS3 runs n times to check the availability of all n items.

2. A value of 1 at the symmetrical elements of DDM indicates participation of two services in a cycle. For example: if DM[i, j]=DM[j, i]=1 then $i^{th}$ and $j^{th}$ element has a bidirectional communication. Its practical interpretation is that the two services need to wait for each other to complete their execution.

3. A non-zero value at a diagonal element of $n^{th}$ power of a matrix indicates the participation of n number of services in a cycle.

The first two cases are specific cases of the case listed under 3. The third case is a general case for a cycle of any length ($n$). In case 1 and 3 the value of diagonal elements of the DDM has a key role in cycle identification. From this observation, in the proposed approach we used the third test, which incorporates the special case given in one and two, for identification of cycle of any length $k$.

Testing self loop is trivial. It only requires checking the diagonal elements of the dependency matrix(DDM). But, finding a cycle involving $n$ ($n \geq 2$) services and at the same time specifically identifying the services involved demands the calculation of $n^{th}$ power of a matrix, where $n$ is the dimension of the matrix.

In the following sub-sections some reviews on selected matrix properties and their implication in cyclic dependency extraction are presented. In this regard properties of an adjacency matrix and a power of matrix are investigated.

### 5.2.1 Adjacency matrix

*Definition 5.1* The adjacency matrix of a simple graph is a matrix with rows and columns labeled by graph vertices(V), with a 1 or 0 in position ($v_i$, $v_j$) according to whether $v_i$ and $v_j$ are adjacent or not. For a simple graph with no self-loops, the adjacency matrix must have zeros on the diagonal.

The adjacency matrix represents all the paths of length 1. Each entry indicates whether there is a path length 1 between the corresponding nodes or not. It also tells us how many paths of length 1 are there between the two nodes. In our context the adjacency matrix is same as the dependency matrix defined in section 3.4.2. The value DM[$i$, $j$]=0 indicates no dependency between service $i$ and $j$ (no path between $i^{th}$ and $j^{th}$ node) and value DM[$i$, $j$]=1 indicates there is dependency between service $i$ and $j$ (there is path of length 1). Therefore, the self loop which is cycle of length 1 in adjacency matrix context occurs when the diagonal element (which is $i = j$ component) of the matrix has value 1. In our context the condition DM[$i$, $j$]=1 for $i = j$ indicates the existence of cyclic dependency on $i^{th}$ component service. This implies a service is dependent on itself. It also means a service needs to execute more than once to accomplish the part of the requested composite task.

### 5.2.2 Power of matrix

*Definition 5.2* The power $A^k$ of a matrix for a non-negative integer is defined as the matrix product of $k$ copies of $A$:

$A^k = A.A.A....A$ ($k$ times)

The detailed description from mathematical point of view of the relationship between cycle existence and a power of adjacency matrix is presented in [57].

According to [57] an adjacency matrix contains all the information on paths of length 1. A non-zero value $p$ at element $a_{ij}$ (diagonal element) of $n^{th}$ power of a matrix indicates existence of $p$ paths(cycles) of length $n$. Note that when we are especially looking for cycles only values of a diagonal elements($a_{ij}$ for $i = j$) are relevant. But, when referring the general case of both cycles and open paths any element $a_{ij}$ is of interest. For example, if we take adjacency matrix and multiply it by itself ($A^2$) the result shows the number of paths between the node $i$ and $j$of length 2. Consequently, when we look at the diagonal elements it shows the existence of cycle of length 2 that begins and ends at that particular node. Therefore, a cyclic dependency of any length involving $n > 0$ services can be found by calculating $n^{th}$ power of a dependency matrix.

Specifically, the diagonal elements $a_{ii}$ of $A^n$ indicates the existence of $p$ cycles of length $n$ that begin and ends at $i^{th}$ node. All nodes or services that participate in the cycle will have the same non zero diagonal element value. To get and collect the nodes(services) that contribute to the cycle, it is required to look all the diagonal elements. In the simple case, which is one cycle of path length $n$, the number of non-zero diagonal elements and path length ($n$) should be the same. But, when there are more than one separate cycles of length $n$ then the participant nodes will have a value that is an integer multiple of $n$. There is a possibility that multiple laps could be seen in power of matrix, i.e. any node(service) with $n$ cycle could also show $n * i$ cycles, where $i$ is a positive integer. Therefore, one has to find a way to exclude such cases. The maximum length of possible simple cycle is the same as number of node(services). In [57] only the theoretical explanation of power of matrix in relation to cycle from mathematical point of view is discussed. We adopted this theory and applied to composition purpose.

From power of a matrix ($A^n$) one can get all the information on paths of length $n$ including cycles. For example, the on-line shopping scenario has cyclic dependency of length 5 because the fifth power of the DDM (matrix 5.1) ($DDM^5$) has non zero diagonal elements for 5 services (see matrix 5.2). The detailed elaboration can be found in section 5.2.3.

This theoretical explanation on an adjacency matrix and a power of a matrix given above is applied in our approach to identify a cyclic dependency. We derived an algorithm for extracting cyclic dependencies and to regenerate a cycle free dependency matrix.

### 5.2.3 Cyclic dependency extraction procedure

An algorithm (algorithm 4) is derived to find cyclic dependency based on the theoretical explanation given in the preceding section. Algorithm 4 gives a procedure for identifying cycles from DM and regenerating cycle free DM. The algorithm mainly utilizes power of a matrix operation. The pseudocode of it is given in appendix 10.

Our aim is only to find simple cycles from dependency matrix and replace the participant services in the cycle with a single compound node, and regenerate a cycle free dependency matrix with the newly created compound node. This is done in two steps. The first step is self loop extraction. The second step is extraction of cycles with more than one participant service and replacement of the cyclic components with a compound node. The extraction and replacement of cycles with more than one participant service is done iteratively (see algorithm 4).

---

**Algorithm 4** The cyclic dependency extraction procedure

1: Initialize $n = 1$

2: Check the diagonal elements of the original direct dependency matrix.

3: Collect and assign flag to all services with non-zero diagonal element value. The flag will be used to assign loop control flow while generating a process model.

4: Reassign all the diagonal elements to zero. (This helps to eliminate multiple laps and finding the cycles repeatedly. It is equivalent of removing the cyclic path from the graph so that we won't traverse it again.)

5: Multiply the dependency matrix by itself.

6: Increment $n$ by 1.

7: Check the diagonal elements.

8: Collect all the diagonal elements(node or services) with non zero value.

9: If the number of nodes that has non zero diagonal value is equal to $n$ then create one compound node and replace all the participant services with the compound node and go to step 12)

10: If the number of nodes that has non zero diagonal value is greater than $n$ (which is integer multiple of $n$) then there exists more than one cycle of path length $n$.

11: Trace the individual cycle participants using original dependency matrix values and create compound node that replaces each cycle and go to step 12)

12: Regenerate the dependency matrix with the compound node replacement(Algorithm 5).

13: Repeat from 5 to 12 till $n$ equals dimension of the original dependency matrix.

---

Algorithm 5 gives a sub-procedure for regenerating cycle free DM with compound node. The pseudocode code of this algorithm can be found in appendix 9.4

**Algorithm 5** Regeneration of cycle-free dependency matrix sub-procedure

1: Get the compound node components(participant services in the cycle) and the original dependency matrix.

2: Form a matrix with the compound nodes and the services that are not in compound node.

3: Trace on which individual services each compound node is dependent, i.e. by checking on which services each element of a compound node is dependent and assign the cycle-free dependency matrix row values.

4: Trace which services are dependent on each compound node, i.e by checking which services are dependent on each element of a compound service and assign the cycle-free dependency matrix row values.

5: Assign the other cycle-free matrix values from initial dependency matrix values (for individual services).

In the on-line shopping scenario there are two cyclic dependencies. The first one is a self loop. This is the cyclic dependency involving only WS3 which is indicated by diagonal element DDM[3, 3]=1 in the initial DDM (matrix 5.1). The second one is a cyclic dependency involving 5 services (WS7, WS8, WS10, WS11 and WS12). The process of extracting these two cycles using proposed algorithms is summarized as follows:

1. The initial DDM has one non zero diagonal element which indicates that there is a cyclic dependency that involves only one service and that can be identified

using step 2 of algorithm 4. Matrix 5.1 highlights the self loop in the initial DDM of on-line shopping scenario. Then as it is mentioned in step 3 and 4 of the algorithm it is required to remove the self loop indicator found in step 1 in order to exclude multiple paths. So, in this case the diagonal value DDM[3, 3] should be re-assigned to 0.

2. Calculating the power of matrix for k = 2 to 12 and simultaneously checking the diagonal values at each step enables the identification of other cyclic dependencies. The resulting power matrix of DDM (i.e $DDM^k$) shows no diagonal value has non zero value for k=2, 3, 4, 6, 7, 8, 9, 10, 11, and 12. This indicates there is no cyclic dependency that involves 2, 3, 4, 6, 7, 8, 9, 10, 11 or 12 services. However, the diagonal values for the fifth power of the DDM for WS7, WS8, WS10, WS11 and WS12 are non-zero (see matrix 5.2). This shows there is cyclic dependency among these services.

**Matrix 5.1** Direct dependency matrix for on-line shopping scenario

$DDM =$

| | $WS1$ | $WS2$ | $WS3$ | $WS4$ | $WS5$ | $WS6$ | $WS7$ | $WS8$ | $WS9$ | $WS10$ | $WS11$ | $WS12$ |
|---|---|---|---|---|---|---|---|---|---|---|---|---|
| $WS1$ | 0 | 0 | 0 | 0 | 0 | 0 | 0 | 0 | 0 | 0 | 0 | 0 |
| $WS2$ | 1 | 0 | 0 | 0 | 0 | 0 | 0 | 0 | 0 | 0 | 0 | 0 |
| $WS3$ | 1 | 0 | 1 | 0 | 0 | 0 | 0 | 0 | 0 | 0 | 0 | 0 |
| $WS4$ | 1 | 0 | 0 | 0 | 0 | 0 | 0 | 0 | 0 | 0 | 0 | 0 |
| $WS5$ | 1 | 0 | 0 | 0 | 0 | 0 | 0 | 0 | 0 | 0 | 0 | 0 |
| $WS6$ | 0 | 0 | 1 | 0 | 0 | 0 | 0 | 0 | 0 | 0 | 0 | 0 |
| $WS7$ | 1 | 0 | 0 | 1 | 1 | 0 | 0 | 0 | 0 | 1 | 0 | 0 |
| $WS8$ | 1 | 0 | 0 | 0 | 0 | 0 | 1 | 0 | 0 | 0 | 0 | 1 |
| $WS9$ | 0 | 1 | 0 | 0 | 0 | 1 | 0 | 0 | 0 | 0 | 0 | 0 |
| $WS10$ | 1 | 0 | 0 | 0 | 0 | 0 | 0 | 0 | 1 | 0 | 1 | 0 |
| $WS11$ | 0 | 0 | 0 | 0 | 0 | 0 | 0 | 1 | 0 | 0 | 0 | 0 |
| $WS12$ | 0 | 0 | 0 | 0 | 0 | 0 | 1 | 0 | 0 | 0 | 0 | 0 |

**Matrix 5.2** The firth power of direct dependency matrix of on-line shopping scenario

$DDM^5 =$

| | $WS1$ | $WS2$ | $WS3$ | $WS4$ | $WS5$ | $WS6$ | $WS7$ | $WS8$ | $WS9$ | $WS10$ | $WS11$ | $WS12$ |
|---|---|---|---|---|---|---|---|---|---|---|---|---|
| $WS1$ | 0 | 0 | 0 | 0 | 0 | 0 | 0 | 0 | 0 | 0 | 0 | 0 |
| $WS2$ | 0 | 0 | 0 | 0 | 0 | 0 | 0 | 0 | 0 | 0 | 0 | 0 |
| $WS3$ | 0 | 0 | 0 | 0 | 0 | 0 | 0 | 0 | 0 | 0 | 0 | 0 |
| $WS4$ | 0 | 0 | 0 | 0 | 0 | 0 | 0 | 0 | 0 | 0 | 0 | 0 |
| $WS5$ | 0 | 0 | 0 | 0 | 0 | 0 | 0 | 0 | 0 | 0 | 0 | 0 |
| $WS6$ | 0 | 0 | 0 | 0 | 0 | 0 | 0 | 0 | 0 | 0 | 0 | 0 |
| $WS7$ | 1 | 0 | 0 | 0 | 0 | 0 | 1 | 0 | 0 | 0 | 0 | 0 |
| $WS8$ | 0 | 1 | 0 | 0 | 0 | 1 | 0 | 1 | 0 | 0 | 0 | 0 |
| $WS9$ | 0 | 0 | 0 | 0 | 0 | 0 | 0 | 0 | 0 | 0 | 0 | 0 |
| $WS10$ | 1 | 0 | 0 | 1 | 1 | 0 | 0 | 0 | 0 | 1 | 0 | 0 |
| $WS11$ | 3 | 0 | 0 | 0 | 0 | 0 | 0 | 0 | 1 | 0 | 1 | 0 |
| $WS12$ | 2 | 0 | 1 | 0 | 0 | 0 | 0 | 0 | 0 | 0 | 0 | 1 |

Algorithm 5 takes the identified cyclic components of the initial DDM (see matrix 5.2) and generates a cycle-free dependency matrix which is shown in the matrix 5.3). This matrix has one compound node (CN1) that replaces WS7, WS8, WS10, WS11 and WS12 of the initial DDM.

**Matrix 5.3** Cycle-free direct dependency matrix for on-line shopping scenario

$DDM =$

| | $WS1$ | $WS2$ | $WS3$ | $WS4$ | $WS5$ | $WS6$ | $WS9$ | $CN1$ |
|---|---|---|---|---|---|---|---|---|
| $WS1$ | 0 | 0 | 0 | 0 | 0 | 0 | 0 | 0 |
| $WS2$ | 1 | 0 | 0 | 0 | 0 | 0 | 0 | 0 |
| $WS3$ | 1 | 0 | 0 | 0 | 0 | 0 | 0 | 0 |
| $WS4$ | 1 | 0 | 0 | 0 | 0 | 0 | 0 | 0 |
| $WS5$ | 1 | 0 | 0 | 0 | 0 | 0 | 0 | 0 |
| $WS6$ | 0 | 0 | 1 | 0 | 0 | 0 | 0 | 0 |
| $WS9$ | 0 | 1 | 0 | 0 | 0 | 1 | 0 | 0 |
| $CN1$ | 1 | 1 | 0 | 1 | 1 | 0 | 1 | 0 |

After finding the cyclic dependency the necessary control structures should be attached to the respective services. And then the cyclic dependency indicators should be eliminated from the matrix for the next step.

## 5.3 Construction of Explicit Indirect Dependency Matrix(IDM)

The discussion of explicit direct dependency extraction is covered in chapter 4. Algorithm 1 (see section 4.2.2) takes cycle free direct dependency matrix(DDM) as input and does recursive call of algorithm 2 (see section 4.2.2 ) and delivers an indirect dependency matrix (IDM) that does not include any direct dependency(see section matrix 5.4).

**Matrix 5.4** Indirect dependency matrix for on-line shopping scenario

$DDM =$

| | $WS1$ | $WS2$ | $WS3$ | $WS4$ | $WS5$ | $WS6$ | $WS9$ | $CN1$ |
|---|---|---|---|---|---|---|---|---|
| $WS1$ | 0 | 0 | 0 | 0 | 0 | 0 | 0 | 0 |
| $WS2$ | 0 | 0 | 0 | 0 | 0 | 0 | 0 | 0 |
| $WS3$ | 0 | 0 | 0 | 0 | 0 | 0 | 0 | 0 |
| $WS4$ | 0 | 0 | 0 | 0 | 0 | 0 | 0 | 0 |
| $WS5$ | 0 | 0 | 0 | 0 | 0 | 0 | 0 | 0 |
| $WS6$ | 1 | 0 | 0 | 0 | 0 | 0 | 0 | 0 |
| $WS9$ | 1 | 0 | 1 | 0 | 0 | 0 | 0 | 0 |
| $CN1$ | 0 | 0 | 1 | 0 | 0 | 1 | 0 | 0 |

## 5.4 Dependency matrix analysis

The dependency matrix analysis is done using full dependency matrix. The full dependency matrix(FDM) is calculated by simply adding the direct(DDM) and the indirect dependency matrices(IDM). Matrix 5.5 shows the full I/O dependency matrix of the considered scenario. As alternative way the Warshall algorithm could be used to get the full dependency matrix directly from a direct dependency matrix in one step.

**Matrix 5.5** Full dependency matrix for on-line shopping scenario

$DDM =$

| | $WS1$ | $WS2$ | $WS3$ | $WS4$ | $WS5$ | $WS6$ | $WS9$ | $CN1$ | $N2$ |
|---|---|---|---|---|---|---|---|---|---|
| $WS1$ | 0 | 0 | 0 | 0 | 0 | 0 | 0 | 0 | 0 |
| $WS2$ | 1 | 0 | 0 | 0 | 0 | 0 | 0 | 0 | 1 |
| $WS3$ | 1 | 0 | 0 | 0 | 0 | 0 | 0 | 0 | 1 |
| $WS4$ | 1 | 0 | 0 | 0 | 0 | 0 | 0 | 0 | 1 |
| $WS5$ | 1 | 0 | 0 | 0 | 0 | 0 | 0 | 0 | 1 |
| $WS6$ | 1 | 0 | 1 | 0 | 0 | 0 | 0 | 0 | 2 |
| $WS9$ | 1 | 1 | 1 | 0 | 0 | 1 | 0 | 0 | 4 |
| $CN1$ | 1 | 1 | 1 | 1 | 1 | 1 | 1 | 0 | 7 |
| $N1$ | 7 | 2 | 3 | 1 | 1 | 2 | 1 | 0 | |

From the full dependency matrix, which is free of cyclic dependency, we get two straight forward but important indicators that decide the execution priority of services. The indicators (N1 and N2) are given at the last row and last column of matrix 5.5.

The indicators are described as follows:

1. The number of other services that are dependent on a given service (represented by N1).

   This number can be calculated by counting services taking input directly from output of a given service (explicit direct dependency) plus the number of services that have explicit indirect I/O dependencies on it. From the FDM one can get this value by adding each row of the matrix. Table 5.1 summarizes the result of FDDM (DDM plus IDM). The second row (N1) of table 5.1 shows the number

Table 5.1 : Summary of dependency analyser output

| Web services | WS1 | WS2 | WS3 | WS4 | WS5 | WS6 | WS9 | CN1 |
|---|---|---|---|---|---|---|---|---|
| N1 | 7 | 2 | 3 | 1 | 1 | 2 | 1 | 0 |
| N2 | 0 | 1 | 1 | 1 | 1 | 2 | 4 | 7 |

of services dependent on $i^{th}$ service. For example, there are 7 services dependent on WS1. From this indicator it can be reached to a partial conclusion, that is, if more services are dependent on a service then that service has higher priority. Because, when $m$ services are dependent on a service, definitely that particular service should be executed before all $m$ services that are dependent on it.

2. The number of services a given service is dependent on (represented by N2).

   In a similar manner, as the first indicator, this number can also be found by counting the number of services from which a given service takes input directly (direct dependency) plus the number of services a service indirectly depends on. From the FDM one can get this value by summing up each column of the matrix. In table 5.1 the third row shows the number of services the $j^{th}$ service depends on (N2). For example, WS2 is dependent on only one service. From this indicator we can also reach to another partial conclusion that the more services a service depends on the lesser priority that service has. This is because when a service is dependent on $m$ services this indicates that these $m$ services on which that service depends on should be executed before it. Therefore, from a straight forward analysis of input/output dependency we got the two indicators that provide equally valuable information for creating the process model.

## 5.5 Process model generation

Here, we discuss the application of the result of dependency analysis made using the proposed approach for generating a process model with sequential, concurrent and iterative control flows. Moreover, interpretations of results will be given. Two possible process models can be generated using the two numbers described in section 5.4 as a sorting criteria in a simple sorting algorithm. The main logic behind using sorting algorithm is summarizes using four rules as follows:

Rule 1: If WS1 is dependent on less services than WS2 then WS1 definitely is not dependent on WS2 and WS1 can be executed before WS1.
Rule 2: If more services are dependent on WS1 than WS2 then WS1 is not dependent on WS2 and WS1 can be executed before WS2.
Rule 3: If WS1 and WS2 is dependent on equal number of web services (only quatity wise) then WS1 and WS2 are not dependent on each other and WS1 and WS2 can be executed concurrently.
Rule 4: If equal number of services is dependent on WS1 and WS2 then WS1 and WS2 are not dependent on each other and WS1 and WS2 can be executed concurrently.

These possible process models generated are explained as follows:

1. Sorted based on N1:

   This sorting is based on the number of services dependent on a particular service in descending order. (See table 5.2)

2. Sorted based on N2:

   This sorting is done based on how many other services a particular service depends on in ascending order. This is because a service that depends on many services logically should have lower priority compared to service dependent on a smaller number of services. From rule 2 and rule 3 we have seen services with equal value of N1 or N2 can be executed concurrently. In first case WS4, WS5, and WS9 can be executed concurrently. The first case output process model is shown in table 5.2 and figure 5.2. In the second case WS2, WS3, WS4 and WS5 can be executed concurrently. The resulting process model is given in table 5.3 and figure 5.3.

Table 5.2 : Sorted Based on N1 value in descending order

| Web Service | N1 |
|---|---|
| WS1 | 7 |
| WS3 | 3 |
| WS2 | 2 |
| WS6 | 2 |
| WS4 | 1 |
| WS5 | 1 |
| WS9 | 1 |
| CN1 | 0 |

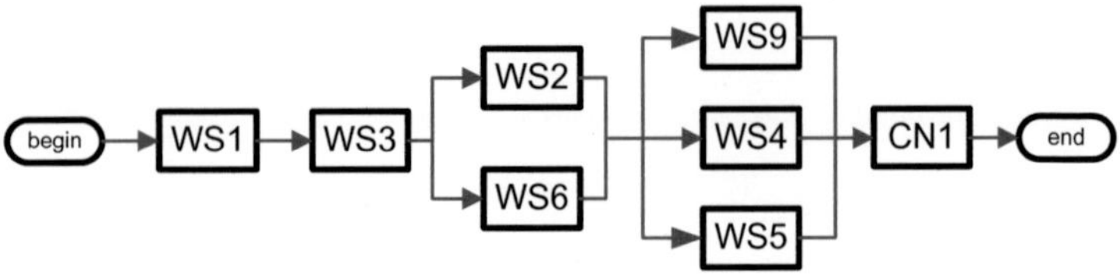


Figure 5.2 : Process model generated based on N1 value(PM1)

Table 5.3 : Sorted Based on N2 value in ascending order

| Web services | N2 |
|---|---|
| WS1 | 0 |
| WS2 | 1 |
| WS3 | 1 |
| WS4 | 1 |
| WS5 | 1 |
| WS6 | 2 |
| WS9 | 4 |
| CN1 | 7 |

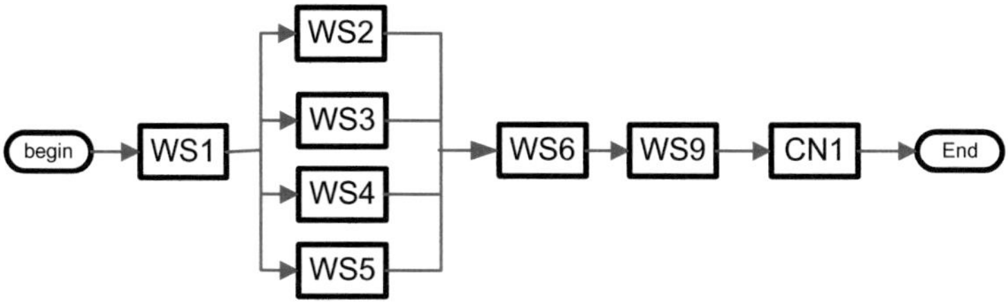


Figure 5.3 : Process model generated based on N2 value(PM2)

Two process models are equally valid and can be taken as two alternative process models.

## 5.6 Chapter summary and discussion

The approach presented in this chapter represents the I/O dependencies as a matrix. The matrix representation enables us to develop an algorithm to extract cyclic dependencies and regenerate and cycle free dependency matrix. Moreover, it allows us to do a simple mathematical analysis which provides two important indicators for the composition plan generation.

The cyclic dependency extraction algorithm has a complexity of O $(n^5)$ . The composition plan generation algorithm complexity is equivalent to the sorting algorithm used that is O $(n * n)$ with $n$ being the number of services. Consequently, the overall approach complexity is equivalent to the cyclic dependency extraction algorithm, which is of polynomial time.

We tested the applicability of the matrix based approach using case studies taken from

[22, 25] and other related papers. In all cases our approach gave a process models that are similar to the ones in the papers reviewed. This has been of assistance to empirically prove the aptness of the process model generated by the proposed method. Further validation of the approach is discussed in chapter 7

The matrix model has already been used by [25] for service composition. Comparing with the method in [25] which uses CLM matrix our approach uses a simple algorithm to generate the process model, which we deem, makes it more efficient especially when the numbers of candidate services are high. CLM based technique does not offer a means to identify cyclic dependencies. The author explicitly mentioned that their approach does not work when there is cyclic dependency.

The simplified nature of the proposed methodology increases its applicability in real world scenarios. We have tested the method at a conceptual level making use of scenarios having from 3 to 11 web services. For these scenarios the output process model was valid. Thus, we intend to extend this approach to be able to find complex parameter dependencies, and for exploring other dependencies, for instance Pre-condition/Effect dependencies, and dependencies caused by user constraints. In addition, extensive experiments run with synthetic web services are done to validate this approach. The experimental results will be presented in chapter 7.

# Chapter 6

# Graph based automatic process model generation

In chapter 5 the dependency matrix based automatic process model generation method is presented that models service dependency using matrix. In this chapter the second proposed approach, which is the graph based automatic process model creation [58], will be presented. To generate the process model (composition plan) this approach utilizes only explicit direct dependency among the abstract service descriptions . The explicit direct dependency extraction procedure make use of semantic similarities between I/O parameters of services as discussed in chapter 4.

As its name indicates, this approach represents the extracted I/O dependencies using a directed graph. This approach recognizes the existence of cyclic dependencies among candidate services. Consequently, a cyclic dependency extraction from dependency graph and a regeneration of acyclic graph is taken as first step during PM generation. Then, execution plan generation is done using modified topological sorting algorithm. The on-line shopping scenario is used to explain the approach.

This chapter starts with the description of the procedure of graph based automatic process model generation. Following that, the detailed explanation of each step with the help of cases from the example scenario is presented. Finally, a summary of the proposed technique and its shortcomings are presented.

## 6.1 Automatic process model generation procedure

The proposed architecture for the graph based automatic PM creation is given in figure 6.1. There are five components in the architecture shown in figure 6.1: a dependency graph constructor, a cyclic dependency extractor, an acyclic dependency graph generator, a dependency analyzer and a process model generator. The tasks of these components can be summarized as follows:

1. **A dependency graph constructor** : construct direct dependency graph from the extracted explicit direct dependencies. (steps for the dependency extraction and the generation of dependency matrix are provided in section 4.2.1).

2. **A cyclic dependency extractor**: find out all cyclic dependencies, if there are any, using the Tarjan algorithm developed by [53] for finding cycles in the directed graph.

3. **An acyclic dependency graph generator** : regenerate a graph by making each cyclic sub graph as one compound node.

4. **A dependency analyzer**:

   (a) calculate the number of services dependent on a particular service by counting incoming edges from the acyclic dependency graph found in step 3 or from the original dependency graph constructed in step 1.

   (b) calculate the number of other services dependent on a particular service by counting the outgoing edges from the acyclic dependency graph found in step 3 or from the original dependency graph constructed in step 1.

5. **A process model generator**: uses a graph traversal algorithm (modified topological sorting) to generate an execution plan based on the calculated values in step 4 and the graph found at step 3 if there is a cycle, if not use the original dependency graph constructed in step 1.

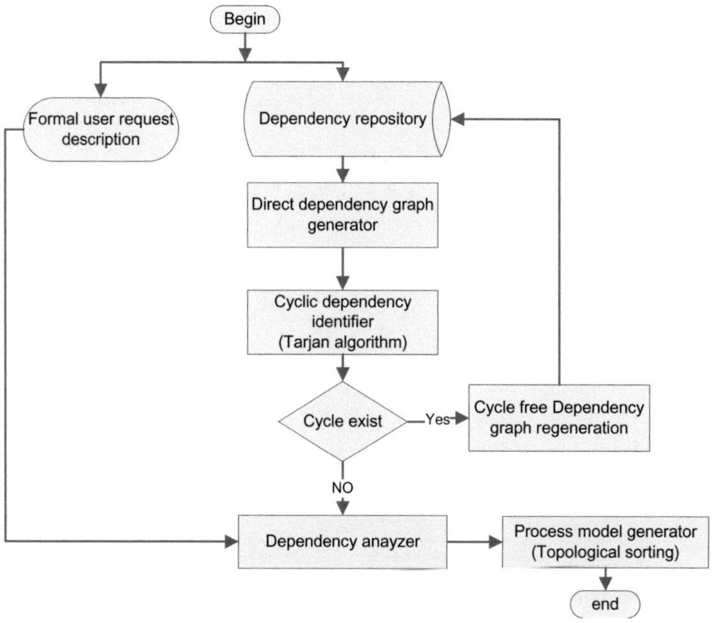


Figure 6.1 : Dependency graph based approach architecture

## 6.2 Construction of dependency graph

As it is mentioned before, in this approach the explicit direct dependency is represented using a directed graph, which can be equivalently represented by an adjacency matrix. Since the detailed explanation of an explicit direct dependency extraction process is presented in chapter 4, here we only explain the way nodes and edges are constructed to represent service dependencies.

The directed graph that represents the dependency among candidate services will have n number of nodes, where n equals to existing number of candidate services. Edges represent the dependency link between services. Since the graph is a directed graph the edge will have a source and a destination node. The service represented by a source node is dependent on the service represented by a destination node. The dependency graph of the on-line shopping scenario is shown in figure 6.2.

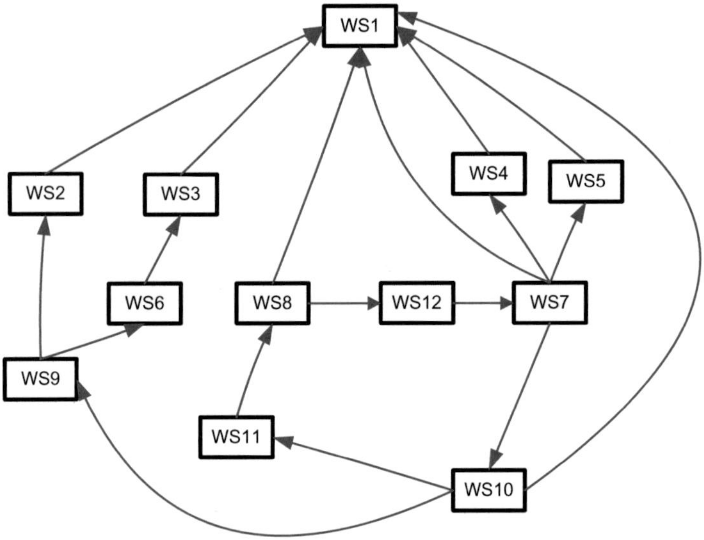


Figure 6.2 : Direct Dependency Graph (DDG)

Note that the data-flow is in the opposite direction to that of the edge direction. This edge direction definition and representation is adopted to show clearly the dependency and a backward graph traversing while generating a process model.

## 6.3 Finding cyclic dependency

To extract the cyclic dependency a modified Tarjan algorithm [53] is used. The tarjan algorithm is originally created to find strongly connected components from a directed graph. This algorithm enumerates all strongly connected components by taking the direct dependency graph(DDG) in the form of an adjacency list. Algorithm 6 shows the pseudo code of Tarjan algorithm. Algorithm 7 shows the pseudo code of main function that makes a call to the Tarjan algorithm to find nodes that are strongly connected to each node. A strongly connected component of a directed graph G includes all set of vertices $V$ such that for all $u$ and $v$ in $V$ there exists a directed path from $u$ to $v$ and from $v$ and $u$. A cyclic component in a graph is strongly connected, and every strongly connected components of a graph contains at least one cycle.

**Algorithm 6** Tarjan algorithm

```
publicArrayList < ArrayList < Node >> tarjan(Nodev, AdjacencyListlist)
v.index = index; //entry level
v.lowlink = v.index; //root of the vertex
v.InSCC = false; v.visited = true; index + +; stack.add(0, v); Noden = null;
for Edgee : list.getAdjacent(v) do
  n = e.to; // for all edges starting from vertex v
  if (n! = null) then
    if !stack.contains(n) then
      tarjan(n, list); //call tarjan for not visited
    end if
    if (!v.InSCC) then
      v.lowlink = Math.min(v.index, n.lowlink);
    end if
  end if
end for
if (v.lowlink == v.index) then
  Node n2;
  ArrayList < Node > component = newArrayList < Node > ();
  repeat
    n2 = stack.remove(0);
    component.add(n2);
    n2.InSCC = true;
  until (n2! = v)
  SCC.add(component);
end if
return SCC;
```

**Algorithm 7** Call of Tarjan to find cycle

**Input:** Dependency graph G(V,E)

$index = 0$ {DFS node number counter}
$S = empty$ { An empty stack of nodes}
**for** *all* $v$ in $V$ **do**
  **if** $v.index$ *is undefined* **then**
    $tarjan(v)$ { Not visited node}
  **end if**
**end for**

Using this theoretical background we used the Tarjan algorithm to identify and extract component services that form a cyclic dependency from a directed service dependency graph. Tarjan algorithm traverses the directed graph in depth first search and collects all strongly connected components that may contain more than one cycle. In our case what we would like to achieve is to identify each simple cycle and regenerate acyclic graph. To effect this, the main function makes a call of the Tarjan algorithm iteratively and the Tarjan algorithm returns cyclic components. The cyclic components returned by the Tarjan algorithm could have single or multiple nodes. A single node occurs when a node does not participate in any cycle or in case of self loop. A multiple node is a result of cyclic dependency that involves more than one node. One call of the Tarjan algorithm returns all possible cycles of a given graph iff the graph is connected. However in case of disconnected graphs, which is possible in case of service dependency, iterative call of the Tarjan algorithm will allow us to have a complete search of cycles from the dependency graph.

Therefore, by considering each cyclic component subgraph identified as one compound node a new acyclic graph can be generated. To do this the Tarjan algorithm ( algorithm 7) is called from any node of DDG. Then, at each return of the Tarjan algorithm with cyclic components the call continues for nodes that are not already visited. In the on-line shopping scenario there is only one cyclic subgraph with 5 services (WS7, WS8, WS10, WS11, WS12). Figure 6.3 highlights the identified cyclic dependency for the scenario.

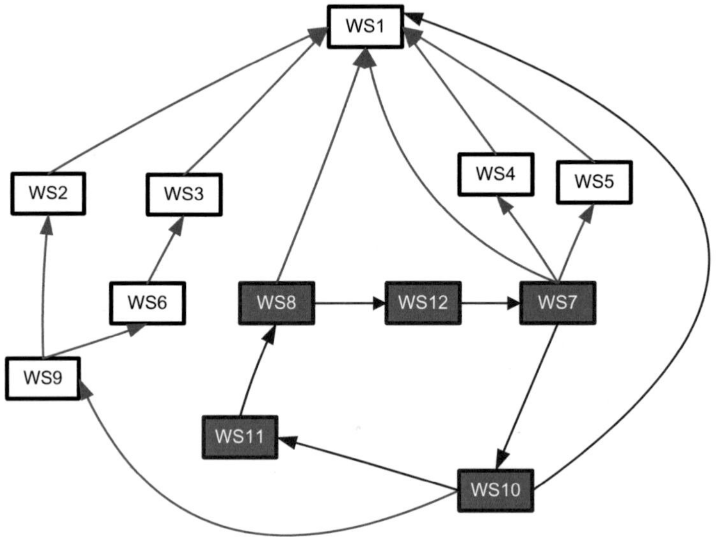


Figure 6.3 : Direct dependency graph with cyclic dependency

After getting all possible cyclic components from the Tarjan algorithm, an acyclic graph generation will continue. This is done by simply replacing the cyclic sub-graph nodes or participant services by a compound node and reconstructing the graph. While constructing the graph, all incoming and outgoing edges to all participant nodes of a cycle should be preserved. This can be done by linking all incoming and outgoing edges of the participant nodes of a cycle to the compound node. In terms of dependency, this means all services dependent on each cyclic component service (services that participate in a cyclic dependency) will become dependent on the compound node that replaces them. Similarly, for all services in which each cyclic component is dependent upon the new compound node also dependent on them. The acyclic dependency graph for the considered scenario generated using the proposed approach is shown in Figure 6.4.

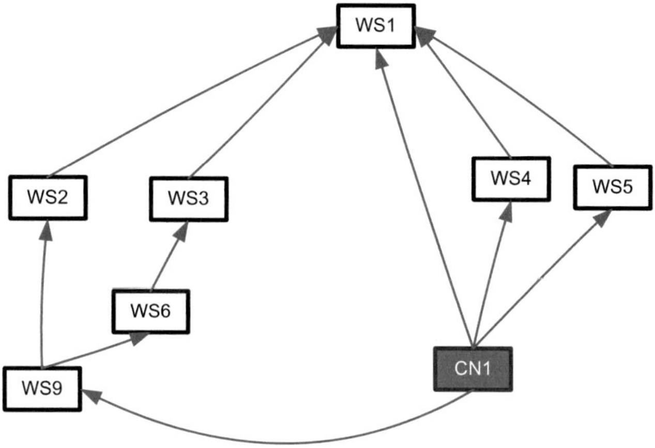


Figure 6.4 : Cycle-free direct dependency graph with compound node

## 6.4 Dependency analysis

From the dependency graph which is free of cyclic dependencies we get two straightforward but important indicators that will be used during a composition plan generation. First, the number of other services that are dependent on a given service (N1), which can be found by counting incoming edges. Second, the number of services a given service is dependent on (N2), which can be found by counting the number of outgoing edges from the dependency graph.

In this approach N1 is used to get services that have higher execution priority. N2 values are used in a service(s) selection criterion that can be included in execution plan. Thus, the two values have a key role in the execution plan generation algorithm.

## 6.5 Process model generation

The composition plan is generated using a topological sorting algorithm. The topological sorting is often used in scheduling jobs or task given precedence constraints. In our case the precedence constraint is the dependency graph. It takes an acyclic graph and outputs a linear ordering tasks (node/services). We adopt modified topological sorting that is used to sort threads that can be executed concurrently [54](see algorithm 8). The composition plan generated by this algorithm for the on line shopping scenario is given in figure 6.5. This execution plan includes a compound node since its input is the regenerated acyclic graph that also has a compound node.

Topological sorting algorithm utilizes the number of incoming edges (N1) and outgoing edges (N2) to generate the composition plan(PATH).

**Algorithm 8** Modified topological sorting

**Input:** Dependency graph G(V,E)

**Output:** PATH($C_0, C_1 ... C_N$) {PATH contains a sequence of group of services}

$L \leftarrow 0$

$C_0 = C_1 = ... = C_N = Empty\ list$ {Ci contains service(s) that can be executed concurrently }

$Path \leftarrow Empty$

**while** V is Non-Empty **do**

  $C_L \leftarrow all\ v\ in\ V\ \ without\ outgoing\ edge$

  $E \leftarrow E - \{all\ E\ that\ start\ from\ v\ in\ C_L\}$

  $Path \leftarrow Path + C_L$

  $L \leftarrow L + 1$

**end while**

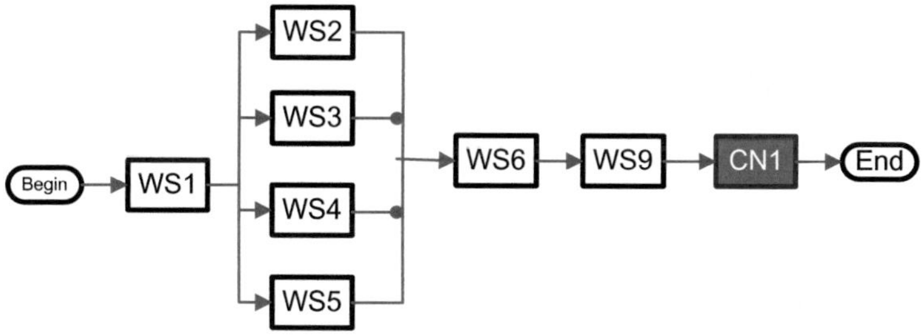


Figure 6.5 : Execution plan with compound node

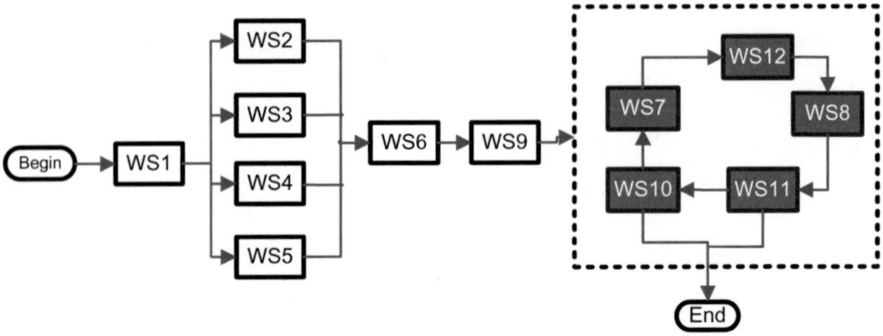


Figure 6.6 : Final execution plan

To get the final execution plan the compound node has to be replaced by the execution plan that involves loop control flow. To do this it is only required to get the starting node of the cycle. Then by traversing the dependency graph in backward direction the order of execution of the WSs that are involved in the loop can be determined. This simplified approach that create execution sub-plan for cyclic component assumes service execution inside the loop is only sequential which is valid in most cases. However, in case of other control flows nested within the loop repetitive use of the topological sorting algorithm is required. The final execution plan generated for the on-line shopping scenario is shown in figure 6.6.

## 6.6 Chapter summary and discussion

In this chapter an Input/Output dependency graph based automated composition plan creation method is discussed. The I/O dependency is represented as directed graph. The usage directed graph enables us to utilize existing graph traversal algorithms to extract cyclic dependencies and generate process model.

The complete graph based approach complexity is determined by the complexity of dependency graph generation algorithm, the cycle extraction algorithm and the process model generation algorithm. The cyclic dependency extraction has the same complexity as the tarjan algorithm, that is of linear in the number of edges (E), vertices (V)and number of cycles(C) of the dependency graph (O(#(V)+#(E)+#(C))). The composition plan generation algorithm complexity is equivalent to the complexity of topological sorting algorithm which is (O(#(V)+#(E))). Since the complexity of dependency graph generation is quadratic time, the overall running time of the graph based algorithm is equivalent to the dominating complexity which is complexity of dependency graph generation.

Similar to matrix based approach the applicability of this approach is tested using case studies taken from [25, 22] and other related papers. In all cases the approach gave process models that are similar to the ones in the papers reviewed. Moreover, we have tested the method at a conceptual level making use of scenarios having from 3 to 11 web services. For these scenarios the output process model was valid. Extensive running experiments are done to further validate dependencies based process model creation method which is presented in chapter 7.

Unlike all other methods that construct dependency between all services in repository we generated dependency between candidate services automatically. We believe, pre-computing all possible semantic links (dependency) between services(even services with same functionality) might lead to extended graph that increases the complexity of plan creation.

# Chapter 7

# Prototype Implementation and Evaluation

In previous chapters, an on-line shopping scenario has been used for the explanation and the conceptual validation of the proposed approaches. In addition, theoretical performance analysis has been conducted in order to specify the worst case complexity of the algorithms of the proposed approaches. However, the conceptual validation alone is not an adequate means to justify the applicability of the approaches in real case scenarios that could have diverse and complex behaviors. The theoretical performance analysis abstracts the implementation details and, consequently, might provide a different result from that of a real performance value. To avert this limitation, we have implemented a prototype performed experiments and evaluated the proposed approaches.

This chapter is devoted mainly for discussions on the implementation and performance study of the two proposed approaches. The chapter is organized as follows, section 7.1 describes the theoretical performance evaluation of algorithms used in the proposed approaches and gives summary of the results from the theoretical (conceptual) evaluation. The conceptual evaluation results will be used as a benchmark for the experimental evaluation. Section 7.2 presents the prototype implementation details together with the discussion of the testbed that facilitates experimental performance evaluation. Section7.3, presents the experimental results and discussion. Finally, the summary and the chapter conclusion will be presented in section 7.4.

## 7.1 Theoretical performance evaluation

The worst-case running time and space complexity of all the algorithms used in both proposed approaches are determined and explained in chapter 5 and 6. The complexity of each algorithm is determined based on the main input factor $n$ (number of abstract candidate web services). Table 7.1 summarizes the explained complexities of both approaches.

Table 7.1 : Summary of theoretical computational complexity

| | MBA | | GBA | |
|---|---|---|---|---|
| | Name | complexity | Name | complexity |
| Direct dependency generation (DDM) | I/O matching | $O(n^2)$ | I/O matching | $O\ (n^2)$ |
| Cycle checker | New | $O(n^4)$ | Tarjan_algorithm | $O(\mid V \mid + \mid E \mid)$ |
| Cycle-free DDM generator | New | $O(n^2)$ | New | O(n) |
| Indirect dependency matrix generator | Floyd-Warshall algorithm | $O(n^3)$ | none | |
| Process model generator | Insertion sorting algorithm | $O(n^2)$ | Topological sorting | $O\ (\mid V \mid + \mid E \mid)$ |
| Overall complexity | | $O\ (n^4)$ | | $O\ (n^2)$ |

$\mid V \mid = n$ is the number of nodes which is the same as number of abstract level component web services

$\mid E \mid$ is number of edges which is the same as number of direct dependencies.

The overall running time complexity of the matrix based approach is of polynomial order of four(4) while the graph based approach has polynomial time order of 2 ( quadratic time complexity). The matrix based approach has a high complexity due to the cyclic dependency checking algorithm.

The space complexity is directly proportional to the data structure used during implementation. Hence, we discuss space complexity by considering pros and cons of possible data structures that can be used. The data structures employed in the two approaches and the resulting space complexities are presented below.

**Matrix based approach**

- **n** : number of services.
- **data structure** : 2 dimensional array
- **complexity**: O($n^2$)

**Graph based approach**

- **n** : number of services or vertices.

  Two possible data representation methods:

- **data structure**: 2 dimensional array
  - complexity: O($n^2$)
  - pro: easy to check if (u, v) an edge in G
  - con: Takes O($n^2$) space if even graph has very few edges;
- **data structure**: Adjacency LIST which can be implemented as an array of (header cells for) or a linked list
  - complexity: O(E) ( each directed edge stored only once)
  - Pro: Linear space and easy to list out all vertices adjacent to u
  - Con: a single adjacent node search takes O(E) operation.

The space complexity of the matrix-based approach is quadratic order. Since the approach relies on the matrix representation of dependency, there is no simpler or optional way of representing the dependency other than a 2 -dimensional array. However, for the graph-based approach there are two optional ways of representing the graph. The first one is a 2-dimensional array in a similar manner to that of the MBA which is quadratic space complexity. The second way of representing is an adjacency list, which results in a linear space complexity. An adjacency list is a data structure for representing graphs. In an adjacency list representation all the vertices in a graph and the list of vertices that have edge from these vertices are stored (that is, called vertex adjacency list). As it is shown above, the space complexity is better when a graph is represented by the adjacency list than that of an adjacency matrix. Besides, in the space complexity, the representation could also be influenced by the computational time of the algorithm. That is because data representation facilitates how elementary operations are done inside algorithms.

The main operations that influence the computation time of graph-based algorithms are : finding all adjacent vertices, removing an edge and deleting a vertex. A single adjacent vertex search takes only one operation which is one value checking in case of matrix representation (i.e. $O(1)$). But in case of an adjacency list it takes the number of edge operations adjacent to that node which could be $O(E)$ in worst case. Looking for all neighboring nodes will take an operation of $O(n)$ complexity in case of matrix. But it will be only equal to the number of adjacent nodes ($O(E)$) operations for a matrix representation.

For the topological sorting algorithm, the main operations that influence the computation time are finding all nodes with no incoming edge, removing the nodes and the edges. The first operation (finding all nodes with no incoming edges) will be simpler with adjacency list which takes $O(n)$ time. The adjacency list also makes second and the third operations simpler.

The Tarjan algorithm is built based on a Depth First Search (DFS) technique. When DFS uses an adjacency list for $n$ vertices, the time complexity will be proportional to $O(E+n)$, and with a matrix representation it will have time complexity proportional to $\mathrm{O}(n^2)$. Thus, the adjacency matrix is better not only in terms of the space complexity but also in terms of the time complexity.

## 7.2 Prototype implementation

### 7.2.1 Background

As mentioned before, an alternative way to evaluate the performance of algorithms is through experiment. For an experimental evaluation a real or a synthetic data can be used on the actual hardware. When performing an experimental performance evaluation of service compositions, it is often desirable to measure the performance of the approaches subjected to various aspects of a composition problem. For example, effects of high number of possible services, combining multiple control flows (concurrent, sequential, alternative, or loop) in a process model, and effects of inter-domain service combinations (openness/closeness of the environment) can be assessed.

To conduct such an experimental performance evaluation getting an appropriate web service environment (testbed) is a pre-requisite. However, it is difficult to get a real web service environment with large and various number of composable web services.

Indeed, there are few existing prototypes that generate synthetic web services and provide test-bed for a service composition. For example, [59] propose a test-bed that generates synthetic web services to form a dependency graph. The focus of their testbed is cross-domain chaining and service composition request generation. The test-bed considers composition mechanisms that use the backward or the forward chaining technique and do a service discovery and a process model creation simultaneously. This approach is not applicable for approaches that take a service discovery and a process model generation as two different steps during a composition. [60] presents a testbed called WSben. WSben is created to facilitate service discovery and composition mechanisms. This testbed is suitable mainly for approaches that combine a service discovery and a process model generation during a composition. Both [59] and [60] do not address the issue of cyclic component in their graph model.

The existence of a testbed that provides abstract service descriptions, which are not interconnected, is an important factor for evaluating composition techniques that do a service discovery and a process model generation separately. This actually is the case pertinent to the two approaches proposed in this thesis. None of the existing testbeds meet this requirement. Therefore, there was a need to develop a new testbed for this research.

To summarize, the reasons why we did not use existing web service environments are:

1. Due to an input/output parameter compatibility problems, it was not possible to use available public web services

2. There are no service repositories available with a large number of real composable services.

3. The existing test beds that generate synthetic web services has description of concrete services. But, we want to have service descriptions at an abstract level or as a community service description.

4. This research splits the service discovery and process generation processes and handles them separately. But, existing test beds support only the evaluation of composition approaches that combine a service discovery and a process model generation in a single step.

5. All testbeds did not consider the existence of cycles in their graph model.

Thus, as a part of this research, a prototype is implemented to get a suitable testbed. This prototype has two parts. The first part is called a Synthetic Composable Web-Service GENerator (SCWSGen); and the second part is called a composition plan or a process model generator. The SCWSGen is responsible for generating synthetic web services which can be used to do the experimental performance evaluation of the composition approaches. The composition plan generator is responsible for generating a composition plan or a process model. In the prototype, the composition plan generator is actually the implementation of the two proposed approaches.

However, any other composition approach could also be implemented. Figure 7.1 shows the two layered implementation architecture of the prototype.

Before designing a general architecture for the prototype, a requirement analysis has been done. The analysis aimed on finding answers to the following questions:

1. Which properties of the composition problems are worth testing?

2. What are the major properties of composable web services? and

3. What kinds of tests (validation) are relevant?

As mentioned earlier, scalability is one of the main problems associated with composition approaches that is worth testing. The scalability of any composition approach as a whole is related to either the scalability of a candidate service retrieval process of the requested task, or to the scalability of a composition plan generation algorithm. The latter is the main focus of this research.

Doing scalability testing of a composition plan generation algorithm requires a testbed with a high number of composable services. As a part of this thesis a testbed with a synthetic web service generator is developed. This synthetic web service generator has a parameter pool, a random I/O parameter picker and a deployable WS generator. It generates $n$ sets of composable synthetic web services from individual services.

The validation process not only requires an arbitrary $n$ number of composable services but also scenarios that represent potential real world cases. The success of generating scenarios that represent real world cases depends on the suitability of the employed random parameter selection process. Thus, assumptions and constraints are imposed to guide the random parameter selection process. For setting up suitable assumptions and constraints reference is made to the related work.

For instance, [61] made a survey of available web services to characterize their behaviors. According to their research finding, the number of operations per services is mostly less than five. Moreover, they claim that the number of input and output parameters per operation is also low. [62] make similar analysis on available public web services. According to their analysis more than 77% of available public web services have less than 5 operations and more than 36% of them have only one operation. In their work it is mentioned that, for web services with more than one operation, the possibility of interaction among operations within a service is less. It is also found that there are no compositions among public web services with more than 2 operations [62].

Thus, the following fundamental assumptions and constraints are set based on the above references and also with an intent of simplifying the implementation process:

- the number of operations per service is one,
- a service has on an average three input parameters,
- a service has on an average 2 output parameters,
- $n$ is the maximum number of services to be generated (the number of composable services is a user modifiable constraints),
- $m$ is the number of parameters in a parameter pool (the average total number of parameters proportionally grows with $n$),
- input and output parameters should be picked from the same parameter pool (since the aim is to generate composable web services)

In the next sections, we will discuss the architecture of the proposed testbed.

### 7.2.2 Architecture

The requirement analysis that has been conducted resulted in a two layered architecture (see figure 7.1). The first layer is responsible for generating a generic synthetic web services and for setting-up experimental validation scenarios for the composition approach. This layer generates synthetic web services that have randomly assigned synthetic I/O parameters. The second layer deals with the actual implementation of the proposed composition approaches. In this later layer the proposed composition approaches; i.e. matrix based and graph based approaches, are implemented.

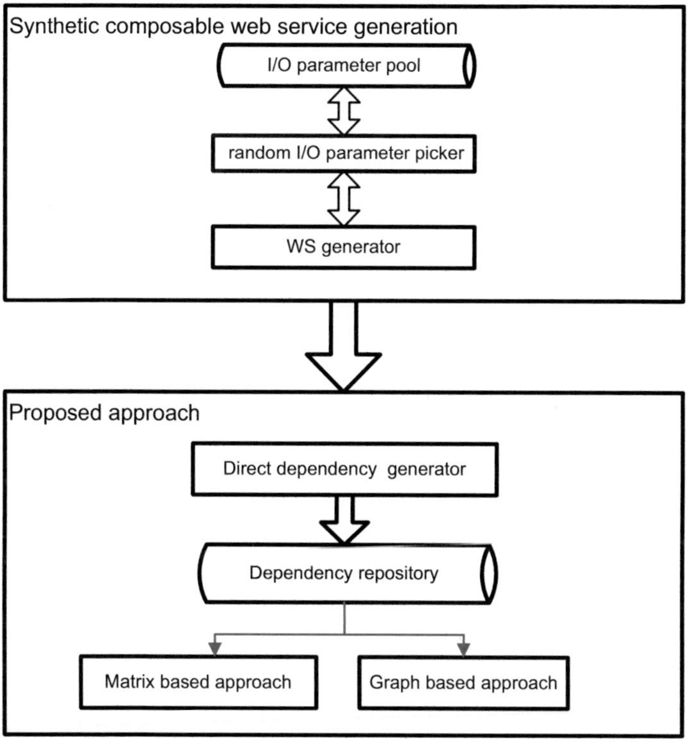


Figure 7.1 : Implementation architecture

For further detailed implementation architecture and the description of each component of the architecture shown in figure 7.1 see appendix 9.

### 7.2.3 SWSgen scenario: demonstrating the prototype

As described before the prototype includes the SCWSGen and the layer that deals with the implementation of the two proposed approaches. The SCWSGen is used to generate $n$ number of service descriptions that form composite service scenarios. Each scenario will contain $n$ number of services that have various numbers of services and dependency arrangement at each run.

The prototype has a graphical user interface (GUI) that takes a user inputs. In order to perform the testing of the proposed approaches a user has to initially provide to the SWSGEn the required number of services ($n$). Then using the other GUI components of the prototype a user is allowed to run each part of both approaches interactively and generate the final process model and see the partial outputs visually.

The major steps for using the prototype to perform experiments are described below.

**Step 1: Synthetic web service and dependency generation**

The GUI is developed using Java Frame. It has three frames. The first frame is the main frame (figure 7.2) and it includes:

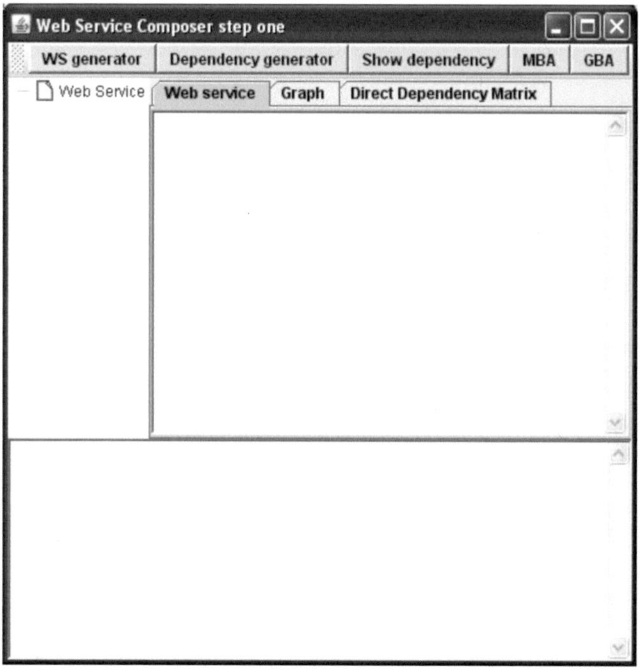


Figure 7.2 : Generating web services

1. Five buttons: web service generator, dependency generator, show dependency, MBA and GBA. These buttons provide a means to receive the action of users' input. The first two buttons allow a user to generate web services and identify dependencies among these web services, respectively. The last two buttons (MBA and GBA) directs the user to the two specific approaches frames. These frames in turn have their own components for taking input from a user and for

generating a process model.

2. Three tabs : web services, graphs and direct dependency matrix. These tabs allow users to see partial outputs, i.e. a dependency matrix and a dependency graph. Since the display area is small the GUI only shows outputs for $n < 40$ but all intermediate and final outputs are stored in file for further use.

3. One JTree component, which is a tree-like structure, is used to display the generated web services names and their inputs and outputs.

To generate synthetic web services a user should provide the number of services to be generated. Clicking "WS generator" button will bring dialog box so that a user gives number of web services. Figure 7.3 depicts the main frame along with the dialog box that prompts a user to input number of services to be generated.

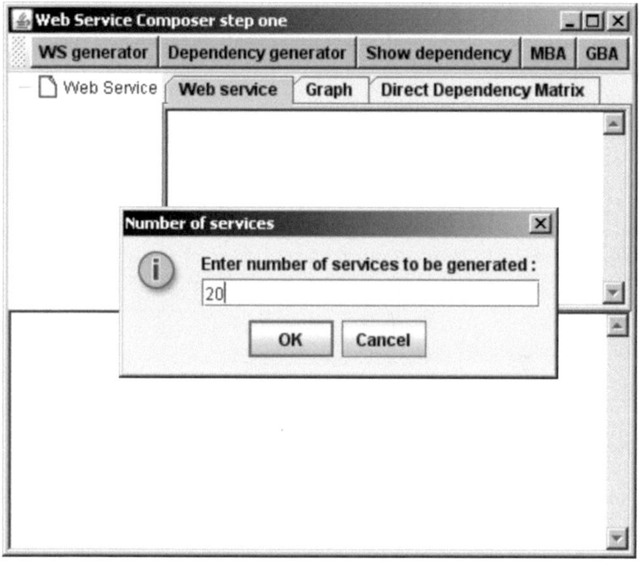


Figure 7.3 : Generating web services

Then Clicking on the "dependency generator" button generates dependency and stores it in a text file. Clicking on the show dependency button displays the dependencies in a graph and a matrix format. The dependency can be seen in a graph format by clicking on the graph tab and it can be seen in a matrix format by clicking on the direct dependency tab. Figure 7.4 shows when the main frame displays the generated web services in the tree format and dependencies in a graph and a matrix format.

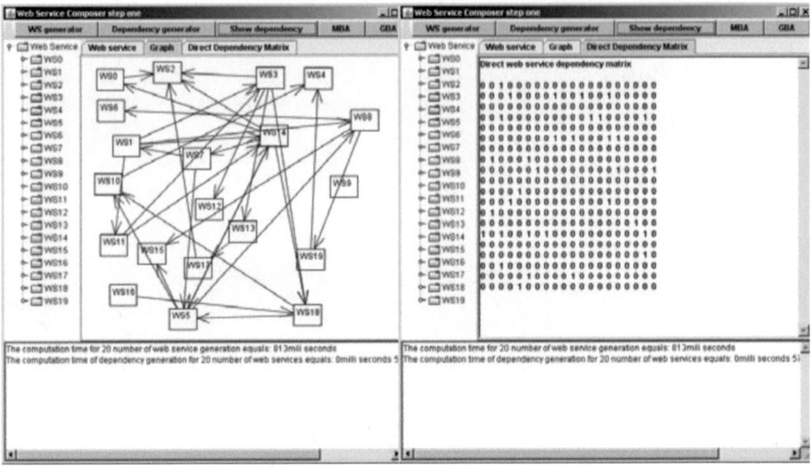


Figure 7.4 : Generating web service dependency.

**Step 2: Dependency analysis and process model generation using MBA**

Clicking the MBA button on the main frame opens a new frame that is connected to the implementation of the matrix based approach. This frame has:

1. Two buttons: cycle check and process model generate buttons. Clicking the cycle check button run the cycle check algorithm and returns with cycle free full dependency matrix. Clicking the process model button generates the final output which is the process model. It displays the process model for $n < 40$ visually and stores the entire result in a text file.

2. Three tabs : cycle, indirect dependency matrix and process model tabs. These tabs allow users to see partial outputs, i.e. the existence of cycle, the indirect,

the full dependency and the final process model respectively. Figure 7.5 shows the matrix based approach implementation frame.

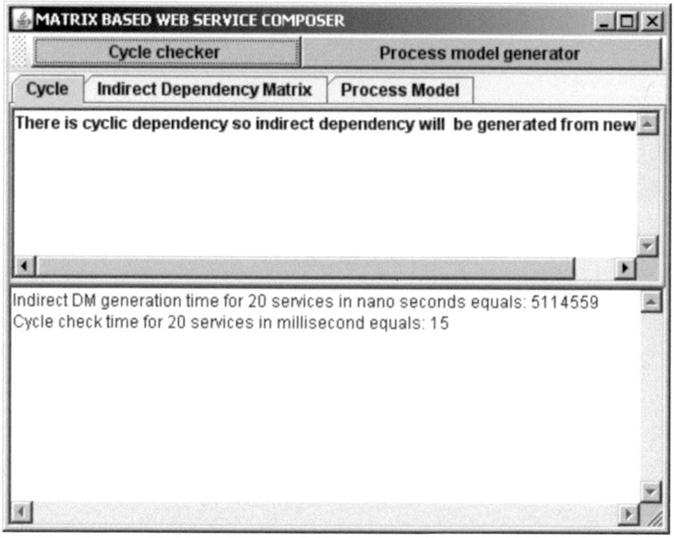


Figure 7.5 : Dependency analysis and process model generation.

**Step 3: Dependency analysis and process model generation using GBA**

Clicking to the GBA button on the main frame opens a new frame that is connected to the implementation of the graph based approach. This frame has:

1. Two buttons: cycle check and process model generate buttons. Clicking the cycle check button run the cycle check algorithm and returns cycle free full dependency graph. Clicking the process model button generates the final output

which is the process model. It displays the process model for $n < 40$ visually and stores entire result in a text file.

2. Two tabs: cycle and process model tabs. These tabs allow users to see the partial outputs, i.e. the existence of cycle and the final process model respectively.

Figure 7.6 shows the graph based approach implementation frame.

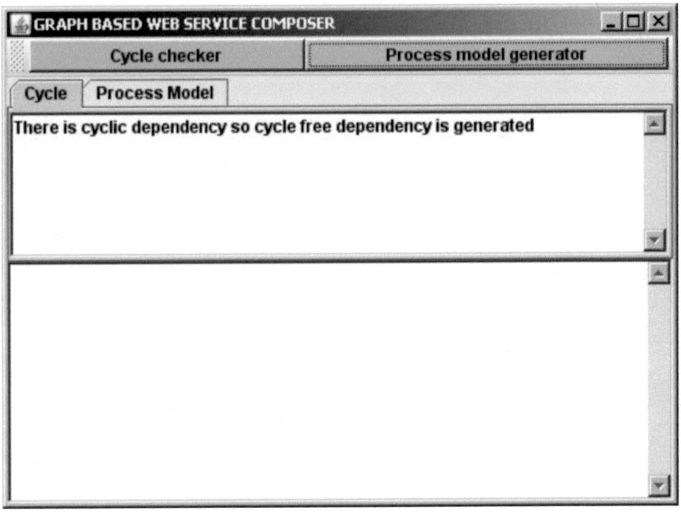


Figure 7.6 : Dependency analysis and process model generation.

## 7.3 Experiments

The experimental performance evaluation mainly focuses on investigating how much the proposed approach is scalable and on monitoring how the proposed mechanisms behave for varying number of services linked by the combination of the different control flows (i.e. loop, concurrent and sequential).

An extensive experimental evaluation is conducted using the web services generated by the SCWSGen. The performance evaluation is done on each component of both approaches as well as on the integral approach as a whole. Then, the experimental results are compared against the theoretical complexities (see section 7.1). Moreover, the comparison of the two proposed approaches using the experimental result is also done. Finally, the assessment of the process model generated by the two approaches is done.

The implementation was performed on the Microsoft Windows XP Professional Edition platform (Service Pack 3)using Java. Apache tomcat was used as a back end server to deploy the web services. The code written for performing the evaluations is around 2800 lines of codes. A laptop computer with an Intel(R) Celeron(R) M (1.4 GHz) CPU and 1 gigabytes of internal memory was used for running the experiments.

7.2 defines the variables and symbols used in this chapter.

Table 7.2 : Symbols and variables

| Variables | |
|---|---|
| $N_{op}$ | Number of operations per an abstract service description (community) |
| $N_c$ | Number of cycles per a composition plan |
| $N_{SperC}$ | Number of services per cycle |
| $N_{Ipara}$ | Number of input parameters per a service description |
| $N_{Opara}$ | Number of output parameters per a service description |
| Performance measurement parameters and functions | |
| Symbols | Descriptions |
| $t_D$ | Time to extract a direct I/O dependency from the service descriptions |
| $t_C$ | Time to check and extract a cyclic dependency |
| $t_{CFD}$ | Time to generate a cycle free dependency |
| $t_{ID}$ | Time to extract an indirect dependency from a direct dependency |
| $T_{MBA}$ | Total composition time for the matrix based approach |
| $T_{GBA}$ | Total composition time for the graph based approach |

### 7.3.1 Experimental results

Table 7.3 shows the common settings for all simulation experiments.

Table 7.3 : Symbols and variables

| | |
|---|---|
| $n$ | 10-150 |
| $N_{op}$ | 1 |
| $N_{Ipara}$ | 0-3 |
| $N_{Opara}$ | 0-2 |
| $N_c$ | 0-3(depending on number of services) |
| $N_{SperC}$ | 1-5 |

Each algorithm in the proposed approaches runs over several experimental sets of web services. For each experimental run the number of services vary from $n$ =10 to 150 with an iteration range of 10. For each run, the number of services($n$) is an input for the SCWSGen. Synthetic services descriptions are generated from a randomly selected I/O parameter. This randomness in selecting the I/O parameters enables the SCWSGen to generate a distinct set of services for every simulation. Thus, to ensure consistency during simulation, we run each algorithm of the proposed approaches 10 times using the same set of services and calculated the average time. Moreover, we run each algorithm 10 times for the same $n$ with various sets of services. The first one is to see how the algorithm scales when the number of services increases. The later one is to see if the algorithm is influenced by the number of dependencies. Therefore, the number of services ($n$) and the number of dependencies ($E$) are the two variables used for evaluation.

The experimental result presentation is organized as follows: first, the experimental results obtained for each algorithm of the proposed approach is presented; then the aggregated experimental results obtained for each approaches is presented and finally the comparison of MBA and GBA approaches in terms of individual algorithms and aggregated results are presented. Note that each algorithm runs on the same set of data because they should run consecutively in order to get the final output process model.

**Experimental result 1: Dependency generation time and number of dependencies**

This experiment is started by generating $n$ number of synthetic web services containing one operation with three input and two output parameters. Then the dependency among these services is generated and the computation time for $n$ services is recorded in a log file. The maximum value of $n$ is 150, which is greater than practically expected in one work-flow. In most related work it is assumed that a single work-flow could contain between 30 and 50 nodes. Figure 7.7 shows the result of this experiment as a scatter chart. In this chart, each point represents the run time of dependency generator in nano-seconds versus the number of services ($n$). The experiment is run 10 times for each $n$ and the average time is taken. The graph has a shape of a quadratic function and this confirms the result of the theoretical performance analysis of the dependency generation algorithm.

As the number of services increase, the dependency generation computation time also grows quadratically. However, as it is mentioned earlier the maximum number of services in a single work-flow mostly do not exceed 50. Thus, it can be concluded that the dependency generator gives a response in a reasonable time.

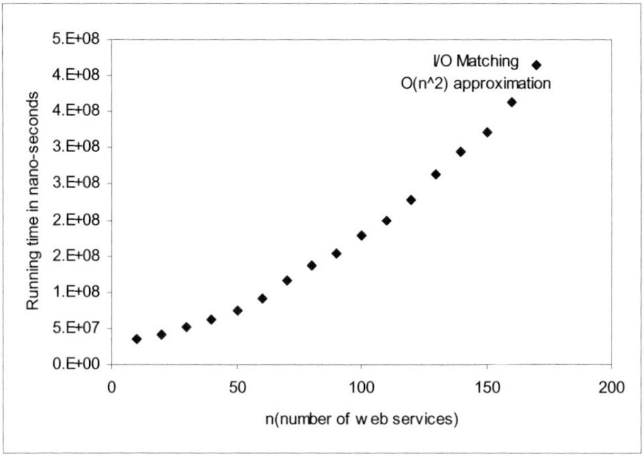


Figure 7.7 : Dependency Generation time vs number of web services

During the experiment of the dependency generation algorithm, a log file is generated. This log file stores the number of dependencies and the number of services for each run. The relationship between the number of dependencies and the number of services is assessed using this information. This is done because the number of dependencies occur among services might influence some of the algorithms of the two proposed approaches. This result enables us to explain the computation time not only based on the number of services but also based on the number of dependencies when necessary.

Here also 10 repeated runs of dependency generator are made, for each $n$ with various sets of synthetic web services. Figure 7.8 is a scatter chart plot of the number of services versus the number of dependencies (averaged over the 10 repeated runs). The chart shows that the number of dependencies is linearly proportional to the number of services. During this experiment, web service and dependency generators run 10 times for the same $n$. Each runs results different set of synthetic services with varies number of dependencies due to the randomness of SCWSGen. But, this variation does not have significant influence on the computation time of the dependency generator.

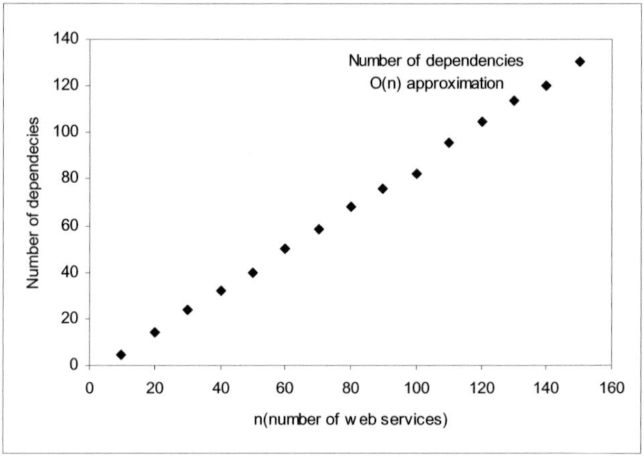


Figure 7.8 : Number of dependencies vs number of web services

### Experimental result 2: Cycle detection time

The cycle detection sub-task is done at the second step for both the matrix and graph-based composition approaches. This experiment uses the dependency among the same synthetic web services generated in the first step of the experiment. Here, the experimental results of cycle detection algorithms of the two proposed approaches is presented. Figure 7.9 and figure 7.10 show the scatter chart of the MBA and the GBA cycle detection algorithms, respectively. The MBA has a higher rate of growth compared to the GBA cycle detection algorithm. This is also observed during the theoretical complexity analysis.

The MBA higher rate of growth comes from the matrix multiplication with three loops that resulted in complexity O($n^3$) and the forth loop running from 1 to $n$ used to find the cyclic path. Thus, the matrix multiplication is carried out $n - 1$ times which makes the overall complexity of MBA cycle detection to O($n^4$).

The Tarjan algorithm is used for the graph-based approach. This algorithm has theoretically a linear time complexity as a sum of the number of services($n$) and the number of edges or dependencies (E) (O ($| n | + | E |$)). But the experimental result indicates it is not fully linear. It is more than a linear complexity and less than quadratic complexity. This is found by calculating the ratio $n^2$ to the computation time from the experimental results. The reason for this difference could be the recursive call of Tarjan algorithm.

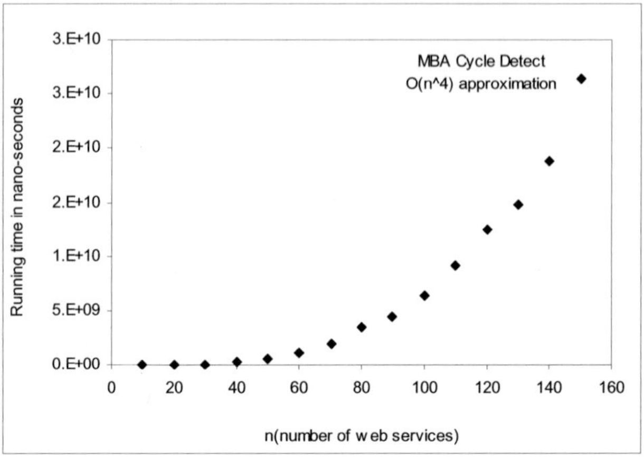


Figure 7.9 : MBA: cycle checking time vs number of web services

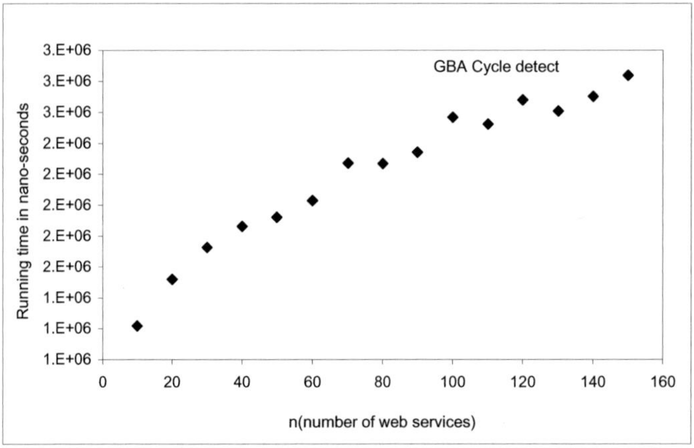


Figure 7.10 : GBA: Cycle detection time vs number of web services

**Experimental result 3: Indirect dependency generation time**

As the graph-based approach does not use an indirect dependency, this experiment is valid only for the matrix based approach. Figure 7.11 shows the scatter chart of the recursive algorithm of the indirect dependency generator (see algorithm 2 in chapter 5). The shape of the graph is similar to a polynomial function of order five.

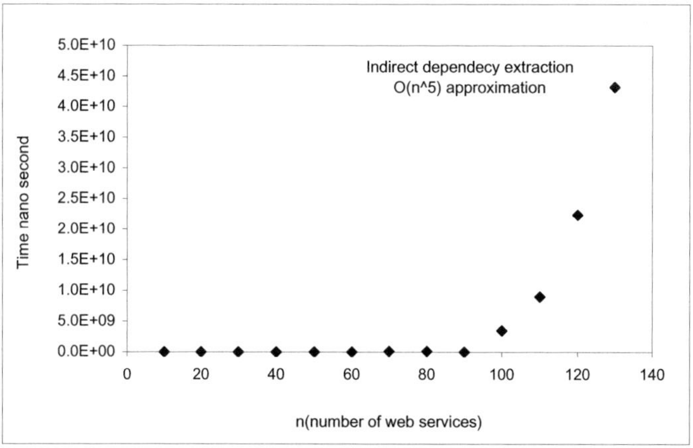


Figure 7.11 : MBA: indirect dependency generation time vs number of web services(recusrsive algorithm)

Figure 7.12 shows the scatter chart of the indirect dependency generator using Warshall algorithm [63]. The shape of the graph is similar to a quadratic complexity function, which is less than that of the result obtained in the theoretical study. This is because though the Warshall algorithm has three loops, the third loop is executed depending on the *if condition* in algorithm 2 line 6 (see section 4.2.2)). This condition is true to the maximum of $n$ times based on the experimental result obtained (see graph 7.8). So the inner loop won't be executed $n$ times with the two external loops.

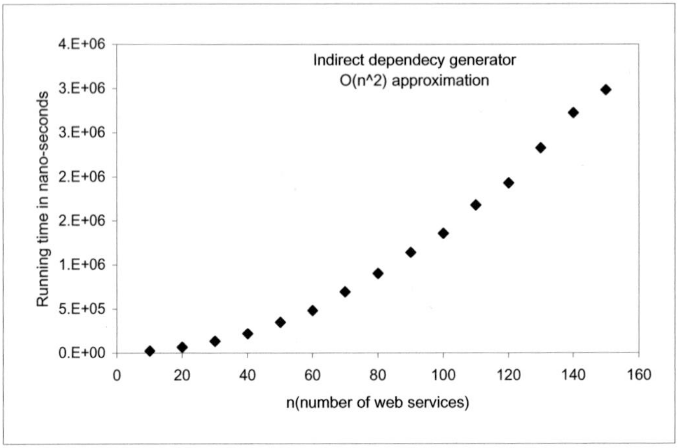


Figure 7.12 : MBA: indirect dependency generation time vs number of web services ( Warshall algorithm)

The two alternative indirect dependency generator have polynomial complexity. Figure 7.13 gives a scatter plot of the two algorithms computation time vs the number of services. In figure 7.13 the y-axis is in logarithmic scale. This graph clearly shows that the Warshall algorithm performace is much better than the recursive algorithm. Therefore, the Warshall algorithm is employed in the matrix based approach.

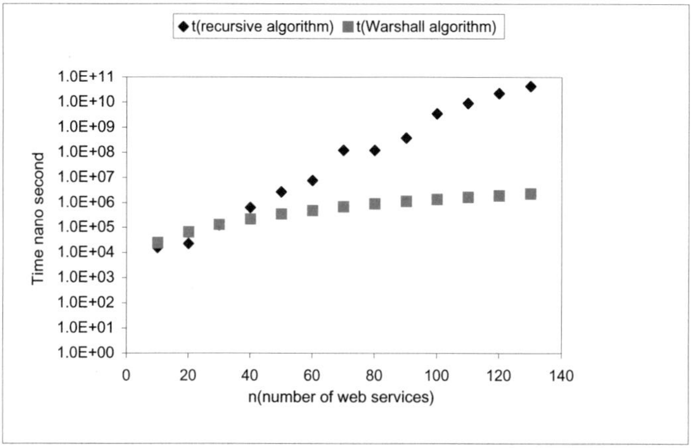


Figure 7.13 : MBA: indirect dependency generation time vs number of web services ( Comparison of algorithms)

**Experimental result 4: process model generation time**

Here the results of the process model generation algorithms of the MBA and the GBA is assessed. In case of the MBA, the experimental results confirm the theoretical result. However, the GBA's topological sorting algorithm experimental result graph has a quadratic time shape. This is because the theoretical complexity assumes that deleting nodes from the graph is a simple operation, but practically it requires $O(n)$ iterations to search and delete a node which is inserted in a path. Moreover, the theoretical complexity does not include the initial graph generation time which has a linear time complexity (see figure 7.14). To clearly see where the process model generator spends most of its time, the initial graph generation time and the path generation graphs are plotted separately. Figure 7.14 shows the initial graph construction time vs the number of services and figure 7.15 shows the composition plan(path) generation part of the algorithm. From these two graphs one can see that there is a significant computation time spent during the initial graph generation. This initial time is spent on file reading and constructing the initial graph. Figure 7.16 shows clearly the percentage of time spent in the two subtasks (graph initialization and path generation) of the process generation algorithms.

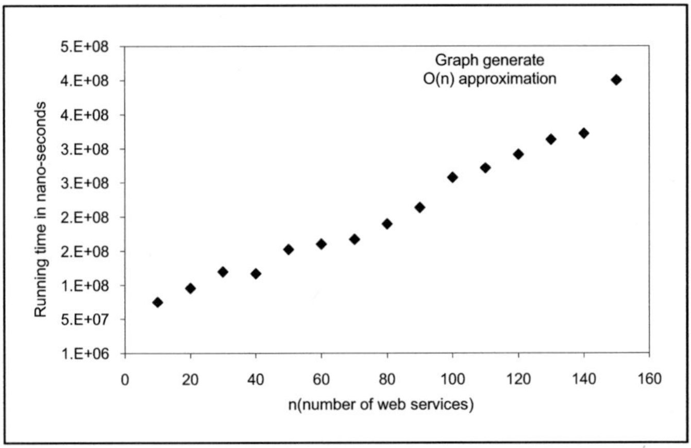


Figure 7.14 : GBA: graph generation time vs number of web services

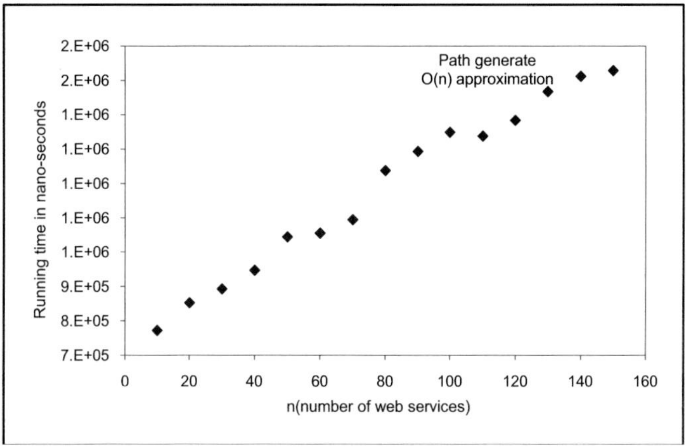


Figure 7.15 : GBA: Process model(path) generation time vs number of web services

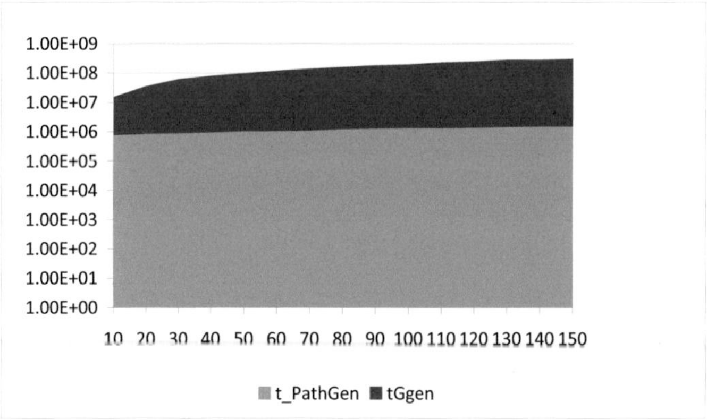


Figure 7.16 : GBA: Ratio of graph generation time to path generation

Figure 7.17 shows the scatter chart of the full process generation algorithm, which is the Topological sorting algorithm, computation time in nano-second versus the number of services.

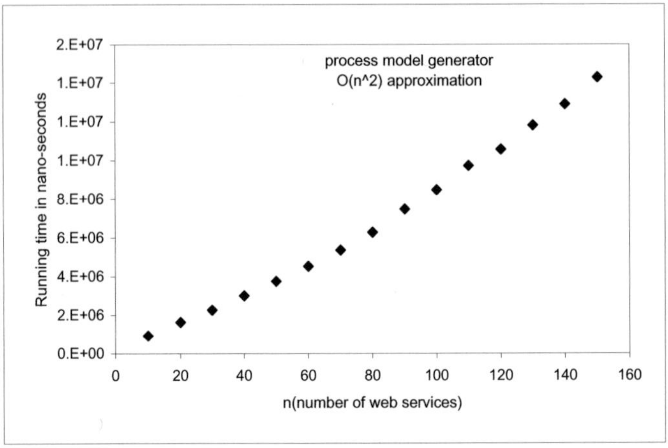


Figure 7.17 : MBA: process model generation time vs number of web services

### Comparison

In this section the matrix and the graph based approaches will be compared in terms of computation time and output process models. Figure 7.18 shows the total computation time of the GBA and the MBA on the same scatter chart. Generally, the MBA computation time is higher than the GBA. As it is discussed before, the main cause of this is that the MBA takes high computation time during cyclic dependency checking. However, the experimental evaluation shows that the MBA has a better response time than the GBA for $n < 30$. In most practical cases, the number of tasks in one work-flow does not exceed 40. We can conclude the MBA performs better and is more applicable.

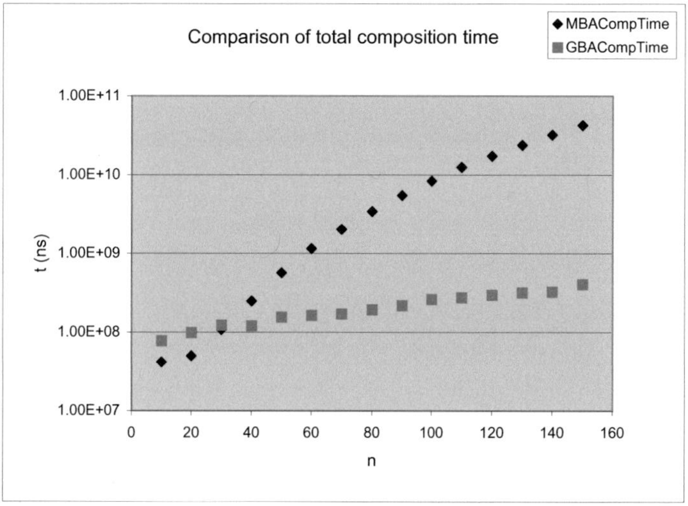


Figure 7.18 : Comparison of MBA and GBA approach: computation time vs number of web services

If we look at the percentage of time spent in each algorithm of both approaches, both the MBA and the GBA spent more time in checking the cyclic dependency. The cyclic dependency checking time is, therefore compared with the other sub-tasks of the composition. Figure 7.19 shows an area graph chart of the trend of the contribution of the cycle detect algorithm and the composition plan generation algorithm. In this graph we used a logarithmic scale to show the results clearly.

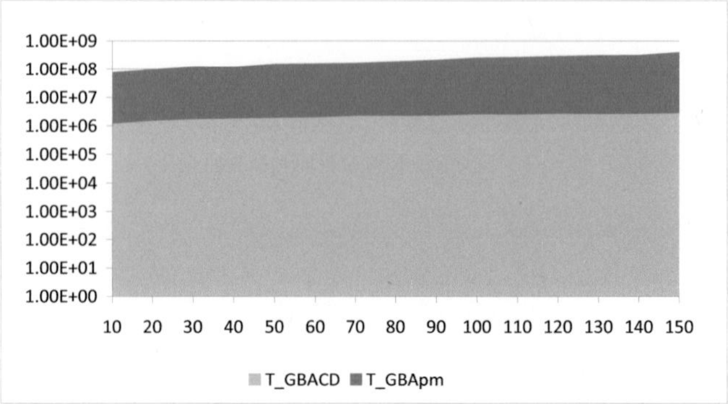


Figure 7.19 : GBA approach: cycle detect and composition plan generation vs number of web services

### 7.3.2 Discussion of performance evaluation results

According to the experimental evaluation reported in this section, it is observed that most of the algorithms experimental evaluation results agree with the theoretical complexity analysis. However, the experimental results of the indirect dependency generator of the MBA, the Cycle checking (Tarjan) algorithm of the GBA, and the process model generator (topological) algorithm are different from the theoretical complexity. The reasons for this difference are:

- the theoretical complexity analysis overlooks some of operations as simple operation which is not practically correct

- the theoretical complexity analysis assumes the worst case, which might not always true. However, the experimental evaluation provides the practical result based on the considered cases.

In section 7.3 the run-time performance of the MBA and the GBA is analyzed and the two results are also compared. From the result it is observed that although the GBA performs well, it has still room for improvement. For instance, the GBA cycle detection algorithm during the experimental study has been found to be quadratic, this requires improvement. As mentioned before, for $n < 30$ the MBA performs better than the GBA, which shows the MBA approach is more applicable for work-flows with 30 tasks or less. In spite of this strength, the MBA also needs some improvement. Specifically the cycle detection algorithm has a complexity of polynomial time of degree 4. Due to this, the whole approach spent most of its time in detecting cyclic dependencies. This suggests that we need to improve or replace the cycle detection mechanism. This task is left as a future work.

### 7.3.3 Discussion on the generated process models

As a final evaluation step the process models generated by the two proposed approaches are assessed and compared. The resulting process model correctness is verified in terms of the correctness of the execution order (temporal order). This verification is done manually by visual inspection of the process models and the service dependency graph/matrix. To illustrate this, three random scenarios having $n = 10, 20$ and 30 web services were generated by the test bed.

Figure 7.20 shows the dependency graph and matrix for the scenario with $n = 10$.

Table 7.4 and 7.20 show the process model generated for the same scenario by the graph based approach and the matrix based approach, respectively. The process models generated by both approaches comply with the dependency pre-requisite shown in Figure 7.20. Thus, the process models are correct in terms of execution order.

**Test case one n=10**

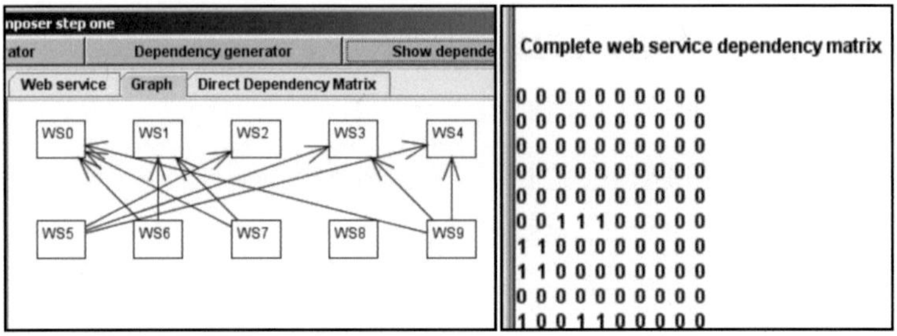


Figure 7.20 : Dependency graph and matrix

Table 7.4 : Output process model from graph based approach

| | | |
|---|---|---|
| 1 | concurrent services level one | WS0, WS1, WS2, WS3, WS4, WS8, |
| 2 | concurrent service level two | WS5, WS6, WS7, WS9 |
| Web services in the same row (level) can be executed concurrently,so are called concurrent web services. | | |
| Web services in row (level) n should be executed before web services in row (level) m, where $m > n$. | | |

Table 7.5 : Output process model from matrix based approach

| | | |
|---|---|---|
| 1 | concurrent services level one | WS0, WS1, WS2, WS3, WS4, WS8 |
| 2 | concurrent service level two | WS6, WS7 |
| 3 | concurrent service level three | WS5, WS9 |

Web services in the same row (level) can be executed concurrently,so are called concurrent web services.

Web services in row (level) n should be executed before web services in row (level) m, where $m > n$.

The process models generated by the matrix-based approach and the graph-based approach are compared. This is again done through a visual inspection of the output process models of the two approaches for the same scenario. To illustrate this the above scenario for $n = 10$ is used, in which case the process model generated by GBA has two sets of concurrent services to be executed, one after the other (see table 7.4). On the other hand, the MBA approach outputs a process model with three sets of concurrent services to be executed sequentially (see table7.5 ). The difference resulted from the logic used in the process model generation algorithms of the two approaches.

The MBA used the number of services a particular service depends upon (N2) as one criterion to sort the services in ascending order and it gets the composition plan with one additional criterion. The second criterion is introduced in order to include concurrent control flow, i.e when services have the same N2, then they become concurrent because two directly or indirectly interdependent services can not have the same value of N2. This process model generator, when it inserts a service in a composition plan, does not have a way to trace whether all services that provide input to a particular service are already in composition plan or not.

In summary, the rules followed by MBA approach are the following:

Rule 1: If S1 is dependent on less number of services (quantity) than S2, then S1 is not dependent on S2, consequently, S1 can be executed before S2.

Rule 2: If S1 is dependent on more number of services (quantity) than S2, then S1 might be dependent on S2, consequently, it is impossible to decide whether S1 can be executed before S2 or not. In such a case to avoid error S1 will come after S2 in the composition plan.

For example, in the process model generated by MBA for $n = 10$, $WS5, WS9$ are in the last concurrent group of services. These two services could be executed along with the second group of services since all their pre-requisite services are in the path. But, their N2 value is 3, which is larger than the N2 value of services in the second group, which is 2. Based on rule 2, WS5 and WS9 come after WS6 and WS7 in the composition plan.

Contrary to MBA, GBA does not have this problem. This is because the process model generation logic, while adding a particular service in the composition plan under construction, has a way to trace weather all pre-requisite services are in the plan or not. Therefore, these problems do not occur. In GBA the process model generation algorithm starts with services that do not depend on any service and keeps on tracing whether all pre-requisite services are included or not. Therefore, the output process model always includes all possible concurrent service executions. As a result, the scenario with $n = 10$ has two sets of concurrent services. Thus, the output process model by the GBA is more condensed than the MBA. This makes the execution time of a composite service created by the GBA less than that of the one created by the MBA, provided that there is enough hardware resource to execute concurrent services.

Figure 7.21 shows the dependency graph matrix for the scenario with $n = 20$. Table 7.7 and 7.6 shows the process model generated for this scenario using the graph based approach and the matrix based approach, respectively.

Figure 7.22 shows the dependency graph matrix for the scenario with n=30. Table 7.8 and 7.9 shows the process model generated for this scenario by the graph based approach and the matrix based approach respectively.

**Test case one n=20**

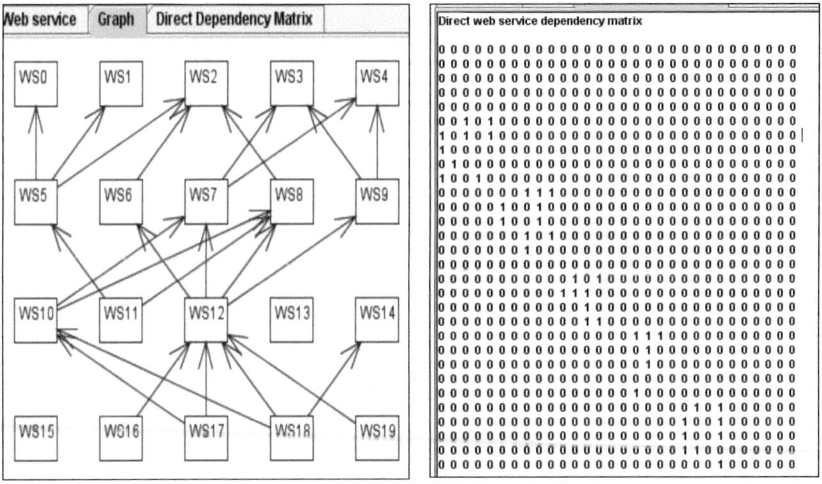


Figure 7.21 : Dependency graph and matrix

Table 7.6 : Output process model from graph based approach

| | | |
|---|---|---|
| 1 | concurrent services level one | WS0, WS1, WS2, WS3, WS4, WS13, WS14, WS15 |
| 2 | concurrent service level two | WS8, WS6 |
| 3 | concurrent service level three | WS9, WS7 |
| 4 | concurrent service level four | WS5 |
| 5 | concurrent service level five | WS10, WS11 |
| 6 | concurrent service level six | WS12 |
| 7 | concurrent service level seven | WS16, WS19 |
| 8 | concurrent service level eight | WS17 |
| 9 | concurrent service level nine | WS18 |
| Web services in the same row (level) can be executed concurrently,so are called concurrent web services. | | |
| Web services in row (level) n should be executed before web services in row (level) m, where $m > n$. | | |

Table 7.7 : Output process model from matrix based approach

| | | |
|---|---|---|
| 1 | concurrent services level one | WS0, WS1, WS2, WS3, WS4, WS13, WS14, WS15 |
| 2 | concurrent service level two | WS5, WS6, WS7, WS8, WS9 |
| 3 | concurrent service level three | WS10, WS11, WS12 |
| 4 | concurrent service level four | WS16, WS17, WS18, WS19 |
| Web services in the same row (level) can be executed concurrently,so are called concurrent web services. | | |
| Web services in row (level) n should be executed before web services in row (level) m, where $m > n$. | | |

**Test case one n=30**

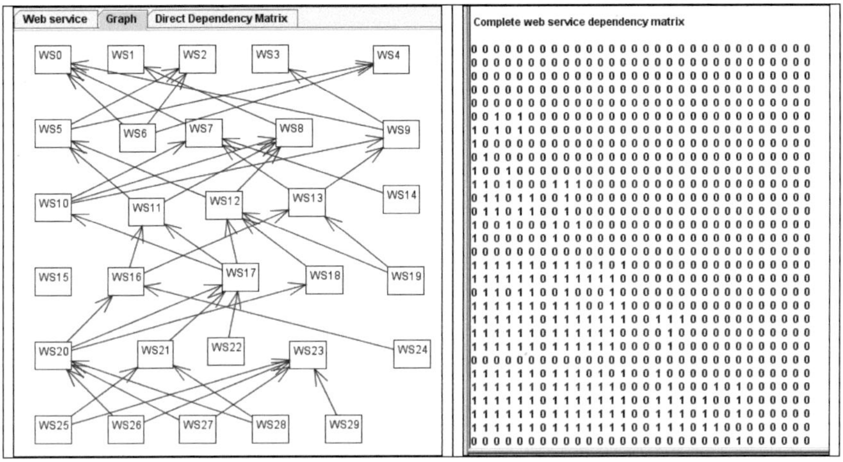


Figure 7.22 : Dependency graph and matrix

Table 7.8 : Output process model from graph based approach

| | | |
|---|---|---|
| 1 | concurrent services level one | WS0, WS1, WS2, WS3, WS4, WS15, WS23, |
| 2 | concurrent service level two | WS5, WS6, WS7W, WS8, WS9, WS29, |
| 3 | concurrent service level three | WS10, WS11, WS12, WS13, WS14, |
| 4 | concurrent service level four | WS16, WS17, WS18, WS19, |
| 5 | concurrent service level five | WS20, WS21, WS22, WS24, |
| 6 | concurrent service level six | WS25, WS26, WS27, WS28, |

Web services in the same row (level) can be executed concurrently,so are called concurrent web services.

Web services in row (level) n should be executed before web services in row (level) m, where $m > n$.

Table 7.9 : Output process model from matrix based approach

| | | |
|---|---|---|
| 1 | concurrent services level one | WS0, WS1, WS2, WS3, WS4, WS15, WS23 |
| 2 | concurrent service level two | WS7, WS8, WS29 |
| 3 | concurrent service level three | WS14, WS5, WS9 |
| 4 | concurrent service level four | WS6 |
| 5 | concurrent service level five | WS13 |
| 6 | concurrent service level six | WS11, WS12 |
| 7 | concurrent service level seven | WS18, WS10 |
| 8 | concurrent service level eight | WS19, WS16 |
| 9 | concurrent service level nine | WS17, WS24 |
| 10 | concurrent service level ten | WS21, WS22 |
| 11 | concurrent service level eleven | WS25 |
| 12 | concurrent service level twelve | WS20 |
| 13 | concurrent service level thirteen | WS27, WS28, WS26 |

Web services in the same row (level) can be executed concurrently,so are called concurrent web services.

Web services in row (level) n should be executed before web services in row (level) m, where $m > n$.

For all cases, outputs of both approaches are valid in terms of execution order, which means no service comes before any other service that is dependent on it (both direct and indirect). Similarly, the output composition plans for $n = 20$ and $n = 30$ of the GBA approach includes all possible concurrent control flows. The MBA approach composition plan has more sets of concurrent services that can be executed concurrently.

## 7.4 Chapter summary and conclusions

### 7.4.1 Summary

The results obtained from the experimental study are comparable to the results from theoretical complexity analysis with the exception of the MBA indirect dependency generator, GBA cycle detection and GBA process model generator. Proper explanation is given for the causes of these exceptions. The overall performance of the proposed approaches can be summarized as follows. First, most of the composition time (for both MBA and GBA approaches) is spent in cycle detection. This step is very important not only for the approaches in this research but also for other approaches which use service dependency information. Second, the number of abstract services which represent a service community with the same functionality and the number of dependencies among such abstract descriptions have impact on the composition time. The bigger the number of abstract services, the bigger is the composition time. Unlike other composition approaches, the number of services within the community does not influence the proposed approaches composition time because the composition is done without considering individual member services. Third, the composition time for MBA is better than GBA for $n < 30$ and for $n > 30$ GBA's composition time is better than MBA. Fourth, output process model of the GBA includes more concurrent control flow than MBA. In this regard, GBA outperforms MBA because the more concurrent services in the process model, the less the the execution time of the composite service.

### 7.4.2 Chapter conclusion

In this chapter, the experimental results and their interpretation is presented. The experimental analysis allowed to validate the theoretical results and made the evaluation of the performance of the proposed approaches possible.

The computation time of dependency generation is checked in relation to the number of services and the number of dependencies. The result indicates that there is no significant change in the computation time with number of dependencies for the same n number of services. Moreover, a test is done to investigate the relationship between number of services and number of dependencies. This information is important for algorithm complexity analysis. The relationship between the number of services and the corresponding dependencies is extracted by calculating the average number of dependencies for a single set of services. i.e. the number of dependencies that exist in one scenario with n number of services.

The MBA spent most of the time in cycle detection. Thus, we believe improving the MBA cycle detection algorithm is one way to improve its performance. One way of achieving this can be using the Tarjan algorithm for cycle detection. This algorithm is used in the GBA.

The GBA approach outputs a composition plan with all possible concurrent services. Thus, its output has more concurrent services than the MBA. In general, the GBA scales better than the MBA. However, the MBA approach results in a better performance for $n < 30$.

The test-bed developed as part of this research differs from other existing test-beds because it generates composable discrete abstract service descriptions. This enables performance evaluation and validation of service composition techniques that does service discovery and composition plan generation separately. The testbed allowed us to prove the applicability and the scalability of the proposed approaches.

# Chapter 8

# Conclusions and outlooks

## 8.1 Conclusions

Creating a composite service or an application from component services, which are developed and meant to work independently, brings dependencies among the services involved. Thus, analyzing and tracking of dependencies are important issues in a composite service development and management.

This thesis advocates the potential utilization of service dependency information for an automatic service composition. The research investigates, develops and implements methods for representing, analyzing and utilizing service dependency information for enabling automatic service composition. As a result, first, a top layer architecture with a composition engine for the purpose of automatic generation of composite service is developed. Second, a two-stepped method for automatic process model generation, given a set of candidate web service descriptions, is proposed.

The top layer architecture gives the general picture of dependency- based automatic service composition. We believe that this architecture will allow to consider a service composition problem as a service dependency identification and analysis problem. We argue that semantic description of web services and user requests enable the automatic detection of dependencies between services. This opens ways for developing more flexible and scalable applications from smaller semantically described services. The proposed architecture utilizes the concept of abstract service description, as opposed to the traditionally used concrete service description. An abstract service description is a way of describing services that have the same functionality (which are also called community services) with a single description. This consolidated abstract service description reduces the size of the service repository and minimizes the search space, which in turn increases the scalability of the service composition and discovery approaches.

The actual realization of the proposed architecture dealt with the following major issues: (i) extracting direct dependencies among candidate service descriptions for the composite task, (ii) identifying cyclic dependencies (if there are any) and regenerating cycle free dependency, (iii) analysis of dependency information for a composition plan generation, (iv) generating a composition plan or a process model using the analyzed dependency information. The first issue is handled by utilizing semantically enabled I/O matching technique. For the remaining three issues, we took advantage of matrix-based and graph-based algorithms and concepts and accordingly proposed two approaches.

The first composition approach uses adjacency matrix to represent the dependency among candidate services. The rows and columns of the matrix represent candidate services. In this approach the cyclic dependency is identified and extracted using a new algorithm developed based on the concept of power of a matrix. This cycle detection algorithm has a complexity of polynomial of degree four. The full dependency matrix (direct and indirect dependency) is extracted using the Warshall algorithm which has a theoretical complexity of $O(n^3)$ but the result from the experiment showed that it has a quadratic complexity. The process model generation of MBA utilizes a sorting algorithm that is modified to suit the intended purpose. The modified algorithm outputs a composition plan with concurrent services. The sorting is done based on the number of services dependent on a particular service ($N_1$) in a descending order. The number of services a particular service depends upon ($N_2$) is sorted in an ascending order. The overall complexity of the matrix based approach is of polynomial complexity of degree four. This approach makes use of direct and indirect dependencies.

The second approach represents a dependency using a directed graph. In the dependency graph nodes represent services and direct edges represent dependencies. The graph-based approach identifies and extracts cyclic dependencies using the Tarjan algorithm. In this approach, the composition plan is generated using the Topological sorting algorithm that is modified to the purpose. The modification is made in order to include concurrent services in the output process model. This approach has an overall theoretical complexity of a quadratic order.

The proposed approaches have been successfully validated conceptually using publicly available real scenarios with 7 to 12 services. Moreover, the approaches have been implemented in a prototype that generates composable synthetic web service descriptions and successfully compose up to 200 services. The experimental results confirmed that both approaches output correct process models in terms of execution order.

The performance of the proposed approaches is also studied theoretically as well as experimentally. For the experimental validation and evaluation purpose, a prototype that has a test-bed to generate synthetic composable services is developed. This test-bed can be used with any other composition techniques. For our purpose, the implementation of the two proposed approaches is done as parts of the prototype. The scalability of the two approaches in terms of computation time and validity of output process model are verified.

Results of the comparison experimental evaluation of the two approaches indicated that MBA performs better when the numbers of web services are less than 30. In practice, most composite services do not involve more than 30 services. This suggests that the matrix-based approach performs better in majority of the cases than the graph-based approach. The output composition plan by the graph-based approach includes all possible concurrent services, which is not the case for the matrix based approach. Both approaches recognize the existence of cyclic dependencies and they propose a way of dealing with it. We believe that identifying, extracting cyclic dependency and generating acyclic dependency matrix or graph should be considered as an element of the steps in approaches that utilized service dependency information. The simplified nature of the proposed methodologies increases their applicability in real world scenarios.

Comparing the MBA with the method in [25] which uses CLM matrix, our approach uses a simple algorithm to generate the process model, which we deem, makes it more efficient especially when the numbers of candidate services are high. CLM based technique does not offer a means to identify cyclic dependencies. The author explicitly mentioned that their approach does not work when there is cyclic dependency.

We believe our approach fills an important missing link in existing service composition approaches. This missing link is the ability for automatic process model generation. The proposed approaches automatically outputs a composition plan with sequential, concurrent and loop control flow, given candidate abstract service descriptions for the composite task.

As final remark we suggest to investigate the Tarjan algorithm to improve the performance of MBA.

## 8.2 Outlook

The work in this thesis can be extended and improved in a number of ways in order to further widen its scope and efficiency. We indicated some of the possibilities for practical improvement in different sections of the thesis.

This thesis focused only on the usage of I/O dependency. However including more dependencies could provide more information, which in turn leads to a better composition plan. Thus, the approach could be extended by exploring other dependencies, for example Pre-condition/Effect dependencies, and dependencies caused by user constraints. Moreover, the proposed approaches in this thesis overlook alternative control flow a further analysis is therefore needed to incorporate alternative control flows in process models.

The service dependency extraction uses straight forward I/O matching. But this need to be improved. This improvement can be achieved by including some more annotation in the abstract service description that to limit the search space during match making.

If a service takes or gives more than one input/output to a particular service then the two services will have multiple dependencies. In this thesis the effect of multiple dependencies in a composition plan generation is not considered. Multiple dependencies could be included as a cardinality of dependencies which might help to improve the composition plan. Thus we recommend to further investigate this concept and its application.

In addition, adaptability techniques for a composite service to unforeseen events happening at run-time, such as a change in the service landscape, user request variation (goal variation) and service failure is a requirement. The service dependency information could also be used to develop run-time process adaptation techniques by utilizing a process model re-generation or modification.

# Chapter 9

# Appendices

## 9.1 Matrix based approach detailed architecture

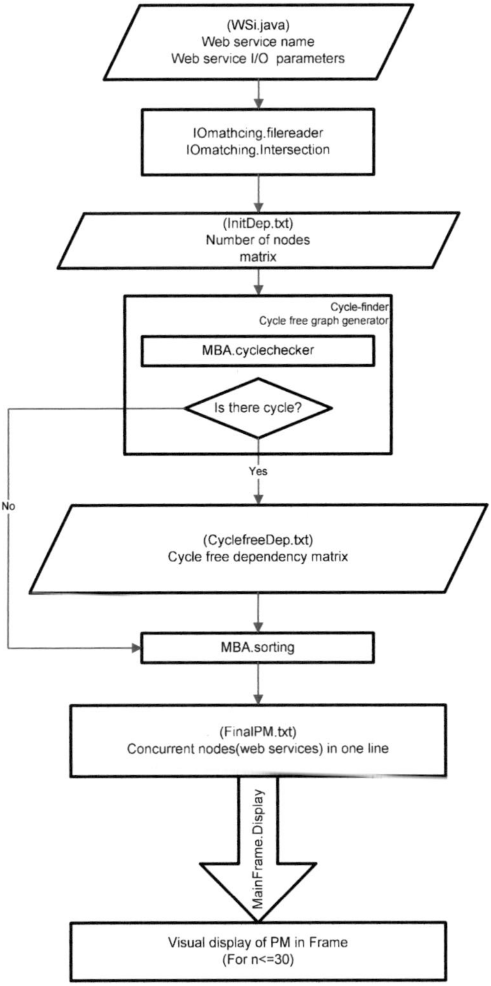

## 9.2 Graph based approach detailed architecture

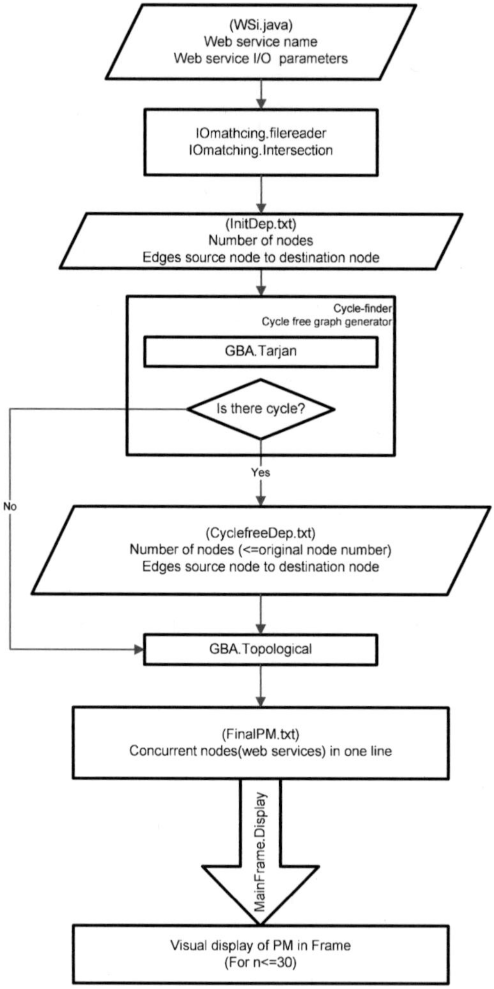

## 9.3 MBA cyclic dependency extraction algorithm pseudocode

**Algorithm 9** The cyclic dependency extraction algorithm in pseudocode

```
Input : DDM
Output: S
PMAT = 1
STACK S = empty
for i = 1 to DDM.size do
    PMAT = PMAT * DDM.M
    for j = 1 to DDM.size do
        if ((PMAT[j, j] = 1)) then
            S.push(DDM.comp(j))
            DDM.comp(j).incycle = true
        end if
    end for
    DDM = Reg(DDM, S, i)
end for
```

## 9.4 MBA cyclic free dependency regeneration pseudocode

**Algorithm 10** The cyclic free dependency regeneration algorithm pseudocode

```
Reg(DDM, S,i)
if (S.size == i) then
    repeat
        CN.addcomp(S.pop)
    until S is empty
else
    K=1
    Create (S.size/i) compound nodes(CN)
    CN[K].addcomp(S.pop)
    while s not empty do
        T=S.pop
        if T dependent with any element CN[K] then
            CN[K].addcomp(T)
        else
            Stemp.push(T)
        end if
    end while
    S=Stemp
    Stemp.clear
    if CN[K].size=i then
        increment K by 1
    end if
end if
NDDM.addcomp(CN)
for i = 1 to DDM.size do
    if (DDM.comp(i)notincycle) then
        NDDM.addcomp(i)
    end if
end for
for i = 1 to NDDM.size do
    for j = 1 to NDDM.size do
        if (NDDM.comp(i) dependOn NDDM.comp(j)) then
            NDDM.M[i][j]=1
        end if
    end for
end for
Return NDDM
```

## 9.5 Synthetic web service generator architecture

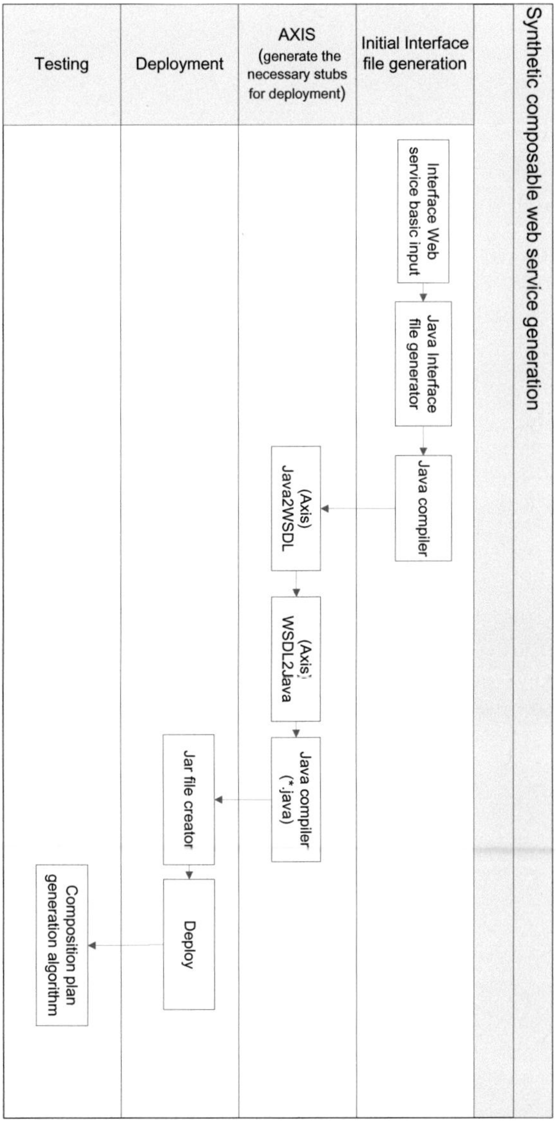

# Bibliography

[1] M. S. S. M. James McGovern, Sameer Tyagi, *Java Web Services Architecture*. Elsevier Science, 2003.

[2] M. Fluegge, I. J. G. Santos, N. P. Tizzo, and E. R. M. Madeira, "Challenges and techniques on the road to dynamically compose web services," in *ICWE '06: Proceedings of the 6th international conference on Web engineering*, (New York, NY, USA), pp. 40–47, ACM, 2006.

[3] A. Alamri, M. Eid, and A. E. Saddik, "Classification of the state-of-the-art dynamic web services composition techniques," *Int. J. Web Grid Serv.*, vol. 2, no. 2, pp. 148–166, 2006.

[4] F. Casati, S. Ilnicki, L.-J. Jin, V. Krishnamoorthy, and M.-C. Shan, "eflow: A platform for developing and managing composite e-services," (Los Alamitos, CA, USA), p. 341, IEEE Computer Society, 2000.

[5] B. Medjahed, A. Bouguettaya, and A. K. Elmagarmid, "Composing web services on the semantic web," *The VLDB Journal*, vol. 12, pp. 333–351, November 2003.

[6] V. Ramasamy, "Syntactical and semantical web services discovery and composition," (Los Alamitos, CA, USA), p. 68, IEEE Computer Society, 2006.

[7] S. R. Ponnekanti and A. Fox, "Sword: A developer toolkit for web service composition," in *Proceedings of the 11th International WWW Conference*

*(WWW2002)*, (Honolulu, HI, USA), 2002.

[8] E. Sirin, J. Hendler, and B. Parsia, "Semi-automatic composition of web services using semantic descriptions," in *In Web Services: Modeling, Architecture and Infrastructure workshop in ICEIS 2003*, pp. 17–24, ICEIS'03, April 2003.

[9] U. Kster, M. Stern, and B. Knig-ries, "A classification of issues and approaches in automatic service composition," 2005.

[10] E. M. G. da Silva, L. F. Pires, and M. J. van Sinderen, "An algorithm for automatic service composition," in *1st International Workshop on Architectures, Concepts and Technologies for Service Oriented Computing, ICSOFT 2007, Barclona, Spain* (E. M. G. da Silva, L. F. Pires, and M. J. van Sinderen, eds.), (Portugal), pp. 65–74, INSTICC Press, July 2007.

[11] S. Mcilraith and T. C. Son, "Adapting golog for composition of semantic web services," in *Proceedings of the Eighth International Conference on Knowledge Representation and Reasoning*, 2002.

[12] S. A. Mcilraith, T. C. Son, and H. Zeng, "Semantic web services," *IEEE Intelligent Systems*, vol. 16, pp. 46–53, 2001.

[13] S. Narayanan and S. A. Mcilraith, "Simulation, verification and automated composition of web services," in *WWW '02: Proceedings of the 11th international conference on World Wide Web*, (New York, NY, USA), pp. 77–88, ACM Press, 2002.

[14] B. Limthanmaphon and Y. Zhang, "Web service composition with case-based reasoning," in *ADC '03: Proceedings of the 14th Australasian database confer-*

*ence*, (Darlinghurst, Australia, Australia), pp. 201–208, Australian Computer Society, Inc., 2003.

[15] G. Kapitsaki, D. Kateros, I. Foukarakis, G. Prezerakos, D. Kaklamani, and I. Venieris, "Service composition: State of the art and future challenges," in *Mobile and Wireless Communications Summit, 2007. 16th IST*, pp. 1 –5, july 2007.

[16] B. Li, "Managing dependencies in component-based systems based on matrix model," in *Proc. Of Net.Object.Days 2003*, pp. 22–25, 2003.

[17] L. Ma, H. Wang, and Y. Lu, "The design of dependency relationships matrix to improve the testability of component-based software," (Los Alamitos, CA, USA), pp. 93–98, IEEE Computer Society, 2006.

[18] S. Basu, F. Casati, and F. Daniel, "Web service dependency discovery tool for soa management," (Los Alamitos, CA, USA), pp. 684–685, IEEE Computer Society, 2007.

[19] J. Zhou, D. Pakkala, J. Perl, and E. Niemel, "Dependency-aware service oriented architecture and service composition," in *IEEE International Conference on Web Services.*, pp. 1146–1149, July 2007.

[20] R. Aydogan and H. Zirtiloglu, "A graph-based web service composition technique using ontological information," (Los Alamitos, CA, USA), pp. 1154–1155, IEEE Computer Society, 2007.

[21] H. N. Talantikite, D. Aissani, and N. Boudjlida, "Semantic annotations for web services discovery and composition," vol. In Press, Corrected Proof, pp. –, 2008.

[22] S. V. Hashemian and F. Mavaddat, "A graph-based approach to web services composition," (Los Alamitos, CA, USA), pp. 183–189, IEEE Computer Society, 2005.

[23] M. Stollberg, U. Keller, H. Lausen, and S. Heymans, "Two-phase web service discovery based on rich functional descriptions," in *In Proc. 4th European Semantic Web Conference (ESWC 2007*, Springer, 2007.

[24] B. Dai and X. Li, "An enhanced goal-based semantic web service discovery," in *Knowledge Acquisition and Modeling, 2009. KAM '09. Second International Symposium on*, vol. 1, pp. 107 –110, 302009-dec.1 2009.

[25] F. Lecue and A. Leger, "Semantic web service composition based on a closed world assumption," *Web Services, European Conference on*, pp. 233–242, 2006.

[26] K. J. Ma, "Web services: What's real and what's not?," *IT Professional*, vol. 7, no. 2, pp. 14–21, 2005.

[27] B. Blau, C. van Dinther, and M. Behrendt, "State of the art in service modeling languages," technical report, Universität Karlsruhe (TH), 2007.

[28] E. Christensen, F. Curbera, G. Meredith, and S. Weerawarana, "Web service definition language (wsdl)," tech. rep., March 2001.

[29] "Oasis, web services business process execution language version 2.0." http://docs.oasisopen.org/wsbpel/2.0/OS/wsbpelv2.0OS.html, 2007.

[30] R. Akkiraju, J. Farrell, J. Miller, M. Nagarajan, M. Schmidt, A. Sheth, and K. Verma, "Web service semantics-wsdl-s," tech. rep., 2005.

[31] J. Farrell and H. Lausen, "Semantic annotations for WSDL and XML Schema," tech. rep., World Wide Web Consortium, August 2007.

[32] M. K. Smith, C. Welty, and D. McGuinness, "Owl web ontology language guide, http://www.w3.org/tr/owl-guide/, accessed," 2004.

[33] U. K. Dumitru Roman, Holger Lausen, "Web service modeling ontology." http://www.wsmo.org/TR/d2/v1.1/D2v120050210.pdf, 2005.

[34] J. De, B. Holger, L. A. Polleres, D. Fensel, J. De, B. Holger, L. Axel, and P. D. Fensel, "The web service modeling language wsml: An overview," 2005.

[35] M. Paolucci, T. Kawamura, T. R. Payne, and K. P. Sycara, "Semantic matching of web services capabilities," in *International Semantic Web Conference* (I. Horrocks, J. A. Hendler, I. Horrocks, and J. A. Hendler, eds.), vol. 2342 of *Lecture Notes in Computer Science*, pp. 333–347, Springer, 2002.

[36] L. Li and I. Horrocks, "A software framework for matchmaking based on semantic web technology," in *WWW '03: Proceedings of the 12th international conference on World Wide Web*, (New York, NY, USA), pp. 331–339, ACM Press, 2003.

[37] J. Rao and X. Su, "A survey of automated web service composition methods," in *In Proceedings of the First International Workshop on Semantic Web Services and Web Process Composition, SWSWPC 2004*, pp. 43–54, 2004.

[38] S. Wang and M. A. M. Capretz, "A service dependency model for multiple service version synchronization.," in *WSE'09*, pp. 7–16, 2009.

[39] Z. Gu, J. Li, and B. Xu, "Automatic service composition based on enhanced service dependency graph," in *ICWS '08: Proceedings of the 2008 IEEE Inter-*

*national Conference on Web Services*, (Washington, DC, USA), pp. 246–253, IEEE Computer Society, 2008.

[40] Q. Liang, L. N. Chakarapani, S. Y. W. Su, R. N. Chikkamagalur, and H. Lam, "A semi-automatic approach to composite web services discovery, description and invocation," *Int. J. Web Service Res.*, vol. 1, no. 4, pp. 64–89, 2004.

[41] Y. Yan, B. Xu, and Z. Gu, "Automatic service composition using and/or graph," in *CECANDEEE '08: Proceedings of the 2008 10th IEEE Conference on E-Commerce Technology and the Fifth IEEE Conference on Enterprise Computing, E-Commerce and E-Services*, (Washington, DC, USA), pp. 335–338, IEEE Computer Society, 2008.

[42] F. Lecue, E. M. G. da Silva, and L. F. Pires, "A framework for dynamic web services composition," in *2nd ECOWS Workshop on Emerging Web Services Technology (WEWST07), Halle*, (Germany), CEUR Workshop Proceedings, November 2007.

[43] V. Agarwal, G. Chafle, S. Mittal, and B. Srivastava, "Understanding approaches for web service composition and execution," in *Compute '08: Proceedings of the 1st Bangalore annual Compute conference*, (New York, NY, USA), pp. 1–8, ACM, 2008.

[44] M. P. Papazoglou, P. Traverso, S. Dustdar, and F. Leymann, "Service-oriented computing: State of the art and research challenges," *Computer*, vol. 40, no. 11, pp. 38–45, 2007.

[45] I. Altintas, E. Jaeger, K. Lin, B. Ludaescher, and A. Memon, "A web service composition and deployment framework for scientific workflows," in *Proceedings*

*of the IEEE International Conference on Web Services (ICWS04)*, 2004.

[46] K. Sivashanmugam, J. A. Miller, A. P. Sheth, and K. Verma, "Framework for semantic web process composition," tech. rep., LSDIS Lab, 2003.

[47] E. Sirin, B. Parsia, D. Wu, J. Hendler, and D. Nau, "Htn planning for web service composition using shop2," *Web Semantics: Science, Services and Agents on the World Wide Web*, vol. 1, no. 4, pp. 377 – 396, 2004. International Semantic Web Conference 2003.

[48] D. Wu, B. Parsia, E. Sirin, J. Hendler, , D. Nau, and D. Nau, "Automating daml-s web services composition using shop2," in *In Proceedings of 2nd International Semantic Web Conference (ISWC2003*, 2003.

[49] S.-C. Oh, D. Lee, and S. R. T. Kumara, "Web service planner (wspr): An effective and scalable web service composition algorithm," *Int. J. Web Service Res.*, vol. 4, no. 1, pp. 1–22, 2007.

[50] D. Berardi, F. Cheikh, G. D. Giacomo, and F. Patrizi, "Automatic service composition via simulation," *Int. J. Found. Comput. Sci.*, vol. 19, no. 2, pp. 429–451, 2008.

[51] A. M. Omer and A. Schill, "A framework for dependency based automatic service composition," in *In Business Process Management Workshops*, p. 535541, Springer, 2008.

[52] A. M. Omer and A. Schill, "Automatic management of cyclic dependency among web services." submitted to ICWE 2011.

[53] R. Tarjan, "Enumeration of the elementary circuits of a directed graph," *J.SIAM*, vol. 2, pp. 211–216, 1973.

[54] Z. Ma, P. Marchal, D. P. Scarpazza, P. Yang, C. Wong, J. I. Gomez, S. Himpe, C. Ykman-Couvreur, and F. Catthoor, *Systematic Methodology for Real-Time Cost-Effective Mapping of Dynamic Concurrent Task-Based Systems on Heterogeneous Platforms.* Springer, 2007.

[55] J. W. Kim and R. Jain, "Web services composition with traceability centered on dependency," vol. 3, (Los Alamitos, CA, USA), p. 89, IEEE Computer Society, 2005.

[56] A. M. Omer and A. Schill, "Web service composition using input/output dependency matrix," in *AUPC 09: Proceedings of the 3rd workshop on Agent-oriented software engineering challenges for ubiquitous and pervasive computing*, pp. 21–26, ACM, 2009.

[57] R. B. FROST, "Directed graphs and their adjacency matrices:misconception and more efficient methods," *Engineering Optimization*, vol. 20, pp. 225–239, 1992.

[58] A. M. Omer and A. Schill, "Dependency based automatic service composition using directed graph," in *Fifth International Conference on Next Generation Web Services Practices*, pp. 76–81, IEEE Computer Society, 2009.

[59] I. Constantinescu, B. Faltings, and W. Binder, "Large scale, type-compatible service composition," *Web Services, IEEE International Conference on web services*, p. 506, 2004.

[60] S.-C. Oh, H. Kil, D. Lee, and S. R. T. Kumara, "Wsben: A web services discovery and composition benchmark," in *ICWS '06: Proceedings of the IEEE Interna-*

*tional Conference on Web Services*, (Washington, DC, USA), pp. 239–248, IEEE Computer Society, 2006.

[61] E. Cho, S. Chung, and D. Zimmerman, "Automatic web services generation," in *42nd Hawaii International Conference on System Sciences, 2009. HICSS '09.*, pp. 1–8, Jan. 2009.

[62] J. Fan and S. Kambhampati, "A snapshot of public web services," *SIGMOD Rec.*, vol. 34, no. 1, pp. 24–32, 2005.

[63] R. W. Floyd, "Algorithm 97: Shortest path," *Commun. ACM*, vol. 5, June 1962.

## Confirmation

I hereby confirm that I am the sole author of this dissertation. This is a true copy of the thesis as accepted by my examiners.

Dresden June, 2011.

Abrehet Mohammed Omer